MW01179171

For God hath not given us the spirit
of fear; but of power, and of love,
and of a sound mind.

2 TIMOTHY 1:7

MY MAGNIFICENT MOUNTAIN

The Journey of Healing

one woman's courage to live and love after divorce

A novelette by
FAY A. KLINGLER

based on a true story

Granite Publishing and Distribution, L.L.C.

Orem, Utah

Portions of this book were adapted from Fay A.
Klingler's book, *The Complete Guide To Woman's
Time.*

This work is not an official publication of The Church
of Jesus Christ of Latter-day Saints. The opinions and
philosophies expressed herein are the responsibility of
the author and do not necessarily represent the position
of the Church.

Library of Congress Catalog Card Number: 97-78279
ISBN: 1-890558-15-X

Production by: SunRise Publishing, Orem, Utah
Printed in the United States of America

To my beloved husband, companion, and friend, Larry N. Klingler, whose charity, gentleness, and integrity warms my heart day to day;

As my legacy to my children, who have taught and buoyed me during our trials;

To my wonderful parents, Miles and June Alldredge, and my brother, Antoine D. Alldredge, and sisters, Diana Ralphs and Jean Smith, who have anchored and sustained me,

And to my marvelous friends and extended family who have provided constant encouragement and support.

Acknowledgments

I express appreciation to Julia Aposhian and Natasha Brown for their help in preparing this book for publication.

Music has a profound power to uplift and heal. Habitually I listened to taped music as I came and went from work during the months I was single and struggling to find a path up my "mountain." The following lyrics are from one of the music pieces I listened to often. They were the inspiration for *My Magificent Mountain.*

Give Me That Mountain

Life on Earth is but a stepping stone
Where we learn to reach beyond the stars.
If we humbly seek, then we will find
Why we're here and who we really are.

Sometimes when I feel alone, and life's road
seems steep and rocky,
I recall a voice from home:
"I want you to come back to me, your Mother
wants you too.
Your brothers and sisters are praying for you."

(Chorus)
If there's a mountain I need to climb,
Give me that mountain—I'll make it mine.

Then I remember times so long ago
And the love I knew before my birth.
"It won't be easy, but I'll see you through"
Was the promise when I came to earth.

When I gaze into the starry skies, I see beyond
into the world hereafter.
That's the time I realize
I want to make it back, I want to be with you.
We're brothers and sisters I'm praying for
you.

(Chorus)
If there's a mountain I need to climb,
Give me that mountain—I'll make it mine.

Chapter 1

An attractive, single woman, and mother of three children, searched for a way to overcome her loneliness and longed to find her purpose and a way to fulfill that purpose.

She wanted to be happy—to feel secure and whole. And she wanted her children to be happy and responsible as well.

Life was frustrating for her because she had tried her best to make herself and others happy—to be a good mother and a loyal wife. But it hadn't been enough. Her husband chose to lie to her, to secretly incur tremendous debt, and ultimately to marry another woman before their divorce was final.

When the single woman was alone, she did not have the confidence and peace of mind she wanted. The hurt ran through her core. She wondered if she would ever discover the secret of healing. She knew enough about real happiness, however, to realize that she must depend on the Lord if she was eventually to find it.

But she wondered how she could find the time to think through her problems with so many responsibilities to carry alone. She was frightened. *How can I survive financially?* she frequently asked herself. *How can I keep my family close? Can I ever heal enough to trust again?*

And so the bright, single woman knelt before the Lord. "Dear Lord, how am I going to make it? Help me find the answers. Please send me help."

The single woman looked for someone who had already found the answers and who might share the secrets with her. Over the next several months, she observed and spoke with many single women: young and old; some with many children, others with only one child or no children, mothers of toddlers and teenagers; those who were bitter and sad about their singleness, and those who seemed to wear it as a proud badge.

She was beginning to see the many ways that others dealt with the challenges and demands of being single.

She noticed many single women who cared about their children. She saw how hard they tried to play the role of father-mother.

She often saw, however, what so many others did not want to see—the results of festering anger, of greed, of compromised values, and the loss of integrity. She often saw defiance or indifference in the eyes of the children; lost hope and confusion in the expressions of the mothers.

She asked one single mother, "How do you make it financially?" The mother said, "You'll learn. . . . Now don't tell my bishop, but the way I do it is I say 'no' to the jobs that bring in too much. You can't make too much money or you won't get the freebies! I cheat just a little when I renew my application for benefits. What you need to do is make it look one way when it's really another. It's not hard. You'll get used to it."

But the single woman knew there was a better way.

She knew the results of a 100%-honest effort were love and peace and joy in the home—for single mothers and children alike.

She continued to speak with other single women. She realized that most women felt as she did. She found only a few single women who appeared genuinely happy. But they were either unwilling or too busy to share their secrets with her.

The single woman wished she could find someone who knew the answers, lived them, and could explain them to her in a useful way.

She believed that a truly happy woman somehow knows how to feel joy in her life regardless of what happens to her. She knows how to teach her children to love life as well. And perhaps most important, she knows she is responsible for her happiness and that when bad things happen, she rejoices in the resources that she has to deal with her pain.

As the single woman continued to talk to others, she began to hear remarkable stories about an older woman. This woman was active and loving life. She always looked happy, and seemed to know how to make others feel happy when they were around her.

The older woman's husband adored her and together they enjoyed a happy family, although the single woman heard it wasn't always that way.

What caught the single woman's attention as she listened to the stories was the fact that Oma, as everyone called the older woman, had at one time also been a single mother. Oma, which means *grandma* in German, had experienced an incredibly traumatic first marriage. After her divorce, and with little education, she and her children worked as a fine-tuned team to miraculously provide for themselves. Years later Oma met and married a wonderful, Christ-like man who also had children. Each of their children had apparently grown into well-adjusted, happy adults.

The single woman wondered if the stories were true. And if they were, would Oma be willing to share her secrets with her.

The single woman heard that Oma and her husband would be the guest speakers at a fireside in a neighboring town. They had recently returned from a foreign country after serving as mission presidents. She found the address in a telephone book and made arrangements to attend.

When the single woman arrived at the fireside, she felt excitement in the air. The building was astir with a cheerful crowd of people overflowing the capacity of the large chapel and cultural hall. Despite the diverse group, she felt unity in the room. It was as if the electrified assembly was a single family joined together for one common purpose—to honor this couple and yet, to be filled and replenished by the warmth of the spirit that radiated the room. The warmth of the spirit felt as tangible as being warmed by a cozy, down comforter on a cold, snowy day.

Many small children sat with their parents in the gray-mauve choir seats on the stand. In the chairs in front of them sat Oma and her husband.

The single woman starred at Oma. She expected to see a more rounded-grandma image. Instead, she was amazed by Oma's vibrant appearance. This attractive woman looked much younger than her years. The single woman wondered, *Could her pattern of being happy have something to do with it?*

Chapter 2

A small child left his chair among the choir seats and cuddled onto Oma's lap. Another child, perhaps the boy's younger sister, quickly followed to sit on Oma's husband's lap. Oma and her husband did not push them away but welcomed them each with a hug. Oma leaned to place a kiss on the little boy's soft cheek. The blonde-haired boy, with the look of delight, returned the kiss. A young mother gathered them back to the choir seats as the meeting began . . .

The single woman watched Oma as she gracefully moved to the podium when it was her turn to speak. Her face radiated peace and tenderness yet confidence and purpose. The single woman thought, *She glows like she knows and lives the gospel. Perhaps she also knows the secret of healing and will help me.*

Oma explained that she and her husband had just returned from Germany. They had been greatly blessed with talented, dynamic missionaries in their mission. She related several short but powerful conversion stories, then humbly said, "I want to tell you about Sister Florentino. When Sister Florentino arrived in the mission, she openly doubted her ability to adequately teach the gospel. German was difficult for her and she became fretful and angry each time she and her companion found their invitations to hear the gospel rejected. At the request of her companion, I met with Sister Florentino.

"She exclaimed with great emotion why she could not be a success in the mission. 'I'm not serving in a good area. If I were in Sister Black's area, I would do well. And I don't think my companion likes me. If I had a different companion I would do better . . . I come from an inactive family you know. If I came from a family like Sister Alldredge, I would have the confidence she has. I could learn the language and be happy.'

"As we visited, I felt Sister Florentino's hopelessness. Then a word came to my mind—*gratitude*. And I recognized the barrier that was keeping her from feeling the sweetness of her mission experience.

"I said, 'Sister, tell me about the things you are grateful for.'

"There was a long pause. Her brown hair hung limp around her bowed face. She slowly lifted her head and stiltedly replied, 'I can't think of anything I'm grateful for right now.'

"She pulled back as I put my hands on her folded arms, but I continued to touch her. 'Sister Florentino,' I said, 'you have forgotten you are a daughter of God and that he loves you. He is aware of your thoughts and actions and the very desires of your heart. You have forgotten that he wants you to succeed and has promised to help you. You have also forgotten that he always keeps his promises.'

"I asked her if she prayed morning and night and if she carried a prayer in her heart through the day. She told me she knelt when her companion knelt, but often closed her eyes and pretended to pray or said words and didn't really think about them. 'He doesn't love me. Don't you see?' she cried. 'It wouldn't be so hard if He loved me.'"

Oma leaned toward the microphone as she continued to relate the story. "I moved a little closer to her, my hand still resting on her arms. 'Sister Florentino, your happiness does not depend on what has happened to you in the past nor on your present circumstances or how others respond to you. Your Heavenly Father *does* love you. Will you accept a challenge from me and honestly work on it?' She cautiously nodded. 'Every morning and every night I want you to kneel in prayer. Don't miss a single day. But I don't want you to say anything until you have thought of at least three things to thank Him for. It may be as simple as thanking Him for the red tulip blooming by your doorstep, or for the alarm awakening you in time to read scriptures. Then I want you to ask the Lord to bless you with the spirit of thanks. Throughout the day remind yourself that you have reserves you cannot imagine—that you *can* succeed. Trust the Lord, blindly at first if you need to. I promise he will comfort you and soothe your challenges. But remember this promise is based on your faithfulness. And faithfulness includes effort. You can't just turn it over to him. Do *everything* you can and then *expect* that he will help you with the rest.'"

Oma squared her shoulders, pausing for a moment as she smiled at the audience. Again leaning toward the microphone she said, "Brothers and sisters, each of us has a mountain. That is God's plan. We're all here to be tested. Every mountain is unique. And I cannot succeed in God's plan for me by climbing your mountain. I have to own and climb my mountain. Sister Florentino took ownership of what she was and where she was headed. In time, even her countenance changed. Her bowed head and sullen expression was no more. She walked with the air of confidence. And her brilliant smile projected a calm assurance that she was not alone. She completed her mission with a marvelous baptism record. But what was most important was that she went home with happiness in her heart and gratitude for her own mountain."

Oma bore her testimony then concluded by referring to the scriptures. "Please read along with me from Doctrine and Covenants 78:17–19."

> Verily, verily, I say unto you, ye are little children, and ye have not as yet understood how great blessings the Father hath in his own hands and prepared for you;
>
> And ye cannot bear all things now; nevertheless, be of good cheer, for I will lead you along. The kingdom is yours and the blessings thereof are yours, and the riches of eternity are yours.
>
> And he who *receiveth all things with thankfulness* shall be made glorious; and the things of this earth shall be added unto him, even an hundred fold, yea, more [italics added].

The single woman heard little of Oma's husband's talk. She sat in a cocoon—everything outside her thoughts was muted and motionless. The things Oma said made sense to her. She thought of the challenge made to Sister Florentino. *I will take that challenge. If Oma is right, my life will be easier, my feelings will heal, and I will be happier.*

A baby's sudden cry for food stirred the single woman to the present as she heard Oma's husband conclude his talk.

"This is our family behind us in the choir seats. They have supported us throughout our mission with love, letters, encouragement, and a strength of independence that has made us feel a team even many miles apart. Today they have come to show their unity in an expression of song—'Count Your Blessings.'"

The family stood and moved closer together. Many held small children in their arms. The blonde-haired boy who earlier sat on Oma's lap for a kiss, scurried to stand by Oma and her husband. The family appeared to be in a joyful, group hug . . .

When upon life's billows you are tempest-tossed,

When you are discouraged, thinking all is lost,

Count your many blessings; name them one by one,

And it will surprise you what the Lord has done . . .

So amid the conflict, whether great or small,
Do not be discouraged; God is over all . . .
Count your blessings;
Name them one by one.
Count your many blessings;
See what God hath done. . . . ("Count Your Blessings," *Hymns,* no. 241.)

Chapter 3

The single woman knelt in earnest prayer each morning and each evening to thank the Lord for her blessings. She prayed for the spirit of thanks.

Over time it did become easier for her to smile and even to laugh when with others. She became fervently grateful for her children. She was thankful for her parents, her brothers and sisters, and her friends. But inside, where others could not see, she still hurt intensely. She feared earning a living alone, and hated leaving her children to go to work. Her loneliness grew.

The single woman yearned to speak with Oma. *Surely there must be something more to the secret of healing than just giving thanks to the Lord,* she thought. She found Oma's telephone number in the directory and called her.

"Oma, my name is Stephanie," the single woman began. "I attended the fireside where you spoke. I've tried to do what you told Sister Florentino to do, but I'm still not at peace. I wonder if I might come and speak with you?"

"Of course Stephanie," replied Oma. "I'd be happy to visit with you." They arranged to meet the next day.

Stephanie felt Oma's smile as she entered the attractive, older woman's home. After they were comfortable over a glass of cool lemonade, Oma asked, "Now, how can I help you?"

Stephanie hesitated and then replied with a question. "Oma, are you happy?"

Oma said with a smile, "Yes, I am happy. But I admit that hasn't always been true. I remember a time when I was very unhappy, when I felt overwhelmed with loneliness and responsibility."

"What made the difference for you?" asked Stephanie. "I have taken the challenge you gave to Sister Florentino. I am grateful for many things. But I resent what my former husband has done to us and cannot heal or find peace. How can I be happy?"

"Stephanie, I do not have all the answers. I just learned a few small secrets," Oma responded in a tender voice, "but they made a very big difference in my life.

"When my previous marriage ended, I moved to Arizona where my parents lived. My brother and one of my sisters lived there also. They were a great emotional support to me. I rented an apartment for me and my children.

"Each morning I arose early and went to a nearby high school track. The narrow ends of the elongated track faced the east and the west. As I ran around the track, the moon gradually set in the sky at one end as the morning sun brightly rose at the other. I often thought how a season of my life had faded away like the moon setting in the west; and that a fresh, new season was erupting like the radiant sun rising in the east. I realized I had to put my past behind me and move forward. I had to take ownership of my mountain, have faith, and lean on the Lord.

"You can't make others' choices for them, Stephanie. Your former husband has his agency to decide his priorities. He has the right to choose his reward by his actions. Really, you don't have any control over anyone but yourself.

"I decided I had to focus on *my* integrity and let my former husband be judged by the Lord.

"I spent that time alone each morning as I ran trying to get to know myself and build my relationship with the Lord. I earnestly worked on being grateful for what he had given me. He had miraculously provided work for me and led me to a wonderful ward family who nurtured me and my children. Through all the terrifying discoveries we experienced, I felt the Lord blessing me with growth, self assurance, tangible work and coping skills, knowledge, and extreme empathy. I even began to thank him for the bad things that happened because I knew he was teaching me to put my priorities where they should be—more tolerant and tender relationships with my family.

"I found that early hour to be the sweetest part of my day; it was my time with Him."

Oma paused to let Stephanie feel the importance of what she was going to say.

"Stephanie, the secret of happiness you're seeking is simply an attitude of gratitude. You choose to be happy. The secret of healing, however, is forgiveness and the passage of time."

"But it is so hard," Stephanie said with a helpless tone. "He doesn't pay the child support. I am afraid I can't hold it all together by myself. I want to be home. I want things to be right for my children."

Oma leaned across the table and softly grasped Stephanie's trembling hand.

"Don't misunderstand me," Oma said, "I know how hard it is—always a lump in the throat, tears that so easily surface, fear of what the future holds, loneliness—oh, yes, I know how hard it is. But I promise you the Lord will not ask more than you can handle."

Oma gently squeezed Stephanie's hand as she rose. She continued talking as she walked to a low, plant-covered bookcase. "You have tremendous reserves you're not yet aware of." Oma took a black, leather-bound Bible from the case and returned to the table. She opened the book to 2 Timothy 1:7. "This is my favorite scripture. I printed it on a poster and hung it on my refrigerator. Read it out loud with me."

Oma's and Stephanie's voices chimed as a duet, "For God hath not given us the spirit of fear; but of power, and of love, and of a sound mind."

Oma continued, "Cling onto the words *power, love,* and *a sound mind.* Focus on your forward movement not the hurt from the past. Pray for help to give up the bitter feelings that frustrate your happiness. Lift up your heart and know you are never alone. Let the Lord comfort you. Lean on him. Trust him. Do all that is in your power, then know the Lord will send you help in one form or another."

A tear landed with a gentle splat on the table in front of Stephanie. She raised her bowed head spilling another small pool of water on her cheek. "Yes, I know," she quietly said. "I asked for him to send me help, and he sent me to you."

Oma stood and drew Stephanie to her feet wrapping her arms around the single woman in a firm hug as she whispered, "The Holy Ghost will guide you. Remember that healing comes one day at a time."

The older woman then looked directly into Stephanie's flooded eyes. "Forgive your former husband, Stephanie. Let him own the mountain he has claimed. Give the hurt to the Lord and move on with power. Focus on bringing the spirit of the Lord into your heart and into your home."

"But I earn so little money. The children, oh, I want to be home," cried Stephanie.

"You can't change what has happened," said Oma. "Paul, in the Bible, told us to lay aside the weight that holds us back and patiently run the race set before us.

"There's a mountain you need to climb. Make it yours. The Lord has promised to see you through. If you do your part, he will always keep his promises."

"But the children . . . ," whispered Stephanie.

"I know," said Oma. "The Lord will bless them too. Talk to them. Tell them all will be well if you work as a team. Show them an example of faith. Develop a budget and let the children know what money you have; allow them the opportunity to assist by working to provide their personal necessities."

Oma continued, "Ask the Lord to bless your children to feel the power of healing; ask him to please heal the hurt."

Then the older woman added, "Several years after my divorce, my son Tim and I were talking about the desperate/blessed experiences we had. . . . Humph," she chuckled. "Tim was about 14 or 15 years old. He said to me, 'It's not been so bad, Mom. I'd rather be a native trout any day.' I asked him what he meant and he told me how hatchery fish are hand fed and consequently smaller and weaker than native fish. He said, 'Native trout grow bigger, stronger, and smarter because they have to fight for everything they have.'

"You and your children will thank the Lord some day for the blessings of growth he has given you," smiled Oma.

"Oma, may I see you again?" asked Stephanie.

"Absolutely," replied Oma reaching for the Bible laying on the table. She pulled a bent, white sheet of paper from the center of the book, folded it, and tucked it into Stephanie's palm. "Call me. I look forward to seeing you again," she said as they walked to the front door.

When inside her car, Stephanie unfolded the wrinkled paper and read:

When you have come to the edge of all the light you know,
And are about to step off into the darkness of the unknown,

Faith is knowing one of two things will happen:
There will be something solid to stand on,
Or you will be taught to fly. (Anonymous.)

Chapter 4

Stephanie met each day with the spirit of thanks and with a prayer in her heart that the Lord would help the hurt to heal for her and for her children. She focused on clearly seeing her mountain and what path she was going to follow to climb it. Often she found herself thinking, *How can I do it all? I'm afraid that skinny thread I'm hanging on to is going to break. How do I hold it together?*

On a clear fall day, the single woman answered the telephone to hear Oma's cheerful voice. "Hello, Stephanie," Oma began. "I just heard about a conference for single parents being sponsored by our stake. I thought you might be interested in the workshops. I jotted down the telephone number for you. You need to register at least two days before the conference and it's being held this Saturday."

"What kind of workshops are they?" asked Stephanie.

"I can't remember all of them. But I remember seeing a couple titles on the poster. One was 'Achieving More Balance in Your Life.' I think another was 'Managing Your Stress.'"

Sounds like just what I need, but how can I go? I don't have the time, thought Stephanie.

"I know what you're thinking," Oma said.

"What?" squirmed Stephanie.

"You're thinking you don't have the time to go."

"That's right," said the single woman. "Saturday is my only day to be home with the children and catch up with the chores. I really don't have the time, Oma."

"I remember feeling that way when I was a single mother. But I finally discovered that I could take better care of my family and chores when I first took reasonable care of myself. Maybe this Saturday could be for you," Oma stated warmly.

The single woman was skeptical but felt an exhilaration. *Perhaps this is what I'm looking for,* thought Stephanie, then she asked, "What is the telephone number?" She wrote down the number as Oma recited it.

The single woman thanked her, looked at the number and decided to call for details. But first she spoke to each of her children to confirm their plans for Saturday and see there were no conflicts with her attending the workshops.

A sunny voice answered the conference registration number. "You can tell at a glance from their titles what the workshops are about. You'll have time to attend two of them. Then there'll be a keynote speaker at the end of the conference. We're trying to decide what rooms to set up depending on how many want to attend each workshop. Can you tell me which you'd like to attend?" the cheerful voice asked as she listed the workshops—"Managing Your Stress, Increasing Your Personal Power, Achieving More Balance in Your Life, Identifying Your Principle and Values, Creating Positive Memories, and Overcoming Your Fears."

The single woman said very slowly, still trying to figure out which workshops would help her the most; she wished she could attend all of them, "I'd like to go to 'Increasing Your Personal Power' and 'Achieving More Balance in Your Life.'"

"That's great," came the buoyant response. "Don't forget to bring your smile. See you at the conference."

Saturday arrived quickly. The conference was well attended. Following the brief opening where instructors were introduced and the time frame and room assignments were explained, the congregation was dismissed to find the first classroom of their choice.

Stephanie entered a nearly full room labeled "Increasing Your Personal Power." A silver-haired, well-groomed woman greeted her by handing her a blue pocket folder and what appeared to be a business card. The front of the card was bordered by embossed, pale blue flowers. Centered on the front of the card was the instructor's name and telephone number. There was a message on the back of the card. It read: *Work your schedule around what is truly important rather than try to work what is important into your schedule.*

To quiet the crowd, the silver-haired greeter moved before them and said loudly, "Good morning my friends. My name is Silvia." The sounds of the crowd muffled. In a quieter but still authoritative voice, the greeter continued, "I printed the name card for you so you could call me if you have any questions. But the saying on the back is more important. Carry it in your wallet or planner to remind you that your future doesn't just happen. You actually invent your future by your personal choices.

"I gave you a pocket folder," she added. "It contains a pencil and some note paper. You'll gain more from today's discussion if you take a few notes, get involved in the exercises, and several times in the coming days reread what you've written."

With an empathetic tone, Silvia stated, "When you are on the survival level . . ."

She's talking to me, thought Stephanie.

". . . and your circumstances deplete the options of how you can use your time, such as when your health is poor or when you are single and a sole provider for a family, you need to keep a clear perspective of what you value most and focus on solutions. These solutions come about as a by-product of what you believe."

Silvia smiled and said, "You've heard it said, 'Your actions speak louder than your words.' Well, it's really true. Your standards, integrity, even your willingness to conform to the Lord's will are reflected in the selections you make of how you use your available time.

"You may say, for instance, your family is the most important thing in the world to you. But is it?" She cocked her head to one side saying, "Are your activities focused on that principle? Do you set time and activities with your family as a priority over *things?*"

After a short pause, Silvia continued, "Imagine you are 93 years old. You are lying on your bed, dying."

A young man, perhaps in his late twenties, sitting next to Stephanie made a grimaced face and a loud groan.

Silvia chuckled along with the crowd, then continued. "Relax," she smiled, "you'll soon *gracefully* pass on to the next life and meet family members and friends.

"As you lie there on the bed, very still, you review and evaluate what you have accomplished in this mortal existence, and what you will be remembered for.

"Let's say you followed the same path you're on right now—the same priorities, the same choices of the use of your time. Looking back, over your 93 years, would you wish to have lived your life any differently?" Silvia asked.

"Well, yah," shouted the man sitting by Stephanie. Others nodded in agreement.

"All right, in that frame of mind, let's do some backtrack planning. Being 93 years old, and ready to pass on, what would you want to be remembered for?" asked Silvia. "What do you really want to accomplish in this life?

"Take a few minutes and write down at least three specific things or experiences that would give you the greatest degree of personal fulfillment to know you have accomplished as you pass on."

Stephanie pulled out a clean sheet of note paper from the blue folder and wrote:

> *To have my children know I love them*
> *For my children and I to have strong testi-*
> *monies of the gospel of Jesus Christ*
> *To have us all active in the Church*

Silvia waited only momentarily then noted, "This past week we had a death in our family. My aunt passed away. I'm grateful my sister and I took the time to go visit her just a couple weeks ago. I would have felt terrible if she had passed away and we hadn't been to see her. I will always remember her as one of my anchors. She was an English professor. She had taught school to provide for her family after her husband died. When her children were nearly all reared, she very successfully remarried.

"I remember her always happy to see me—always willing, actually eager, to feed me (a hungry, single, college student); she took me shopping for clothes (tried to encourage me to wear brighter colors!); she critically edited my first class paper.

"A very busy woman (my aunt was nearly blind), but she never let me believe by anything she ever did that her busyness was more important than I was. I thought I was special to her. The funny thing was, yesterday at the funeral, I found a lot of people thought they were just as special to her! She loved people.

"Here is a copy of her funeral program. She had it all planned before her death." Silvia held the program up in a showing gesture then drew it back as she remarked, "The saying printed on the cover reads, 'You'd better look your best and think your best today.

For today is the sure preparation for tomorrow and all the tomorrows that follow.' (Author unknown.)

"You experience inner peace only when your daily activities reflect your honest, personal values. The more closely you follow God's plan for you, the greater will be your happiness," suggested Silvia.

"Are you taking the time to have personal interviews with your children—private time with each of them? Do you know and visit your neighbors? Do you put relationships first?"

Stephanie turned to her notes and added:

One-on-one time with the kids

Silvia asked, "Do you live by the same rules and standards you preach to your children? Do you set an example of integrity and uprightness, being where you should be when you should be there?"

A blonde-haired woman sitting in front of Stephanie raised her hand as she exclaimed in a negative tone, "But there are only 24 hours in a day! These things take time."

"Yes, that's my point," continued Silvia. "Everything we do, whether it is a task or just a thought, takes time. You control the outcome of your life by controlling your time. You have to allow the leverage of purposely setting long-term goals—goals that are life-fulfilling, goals that fulfill those *most important* things you wrote down. And then you plan time *now*. Pace yourself to the finish so you'll accomplish your goals with your personal priorities in place."

Silvia stated slowly and deliberately, ***"Work your schedule around what is truly important rather than try to work what is important into your schedule.***

"If you need to change your path or pattern of living to accomplish those things you wrote down in our little exercise about dying, you're going to have to be willing to leave your comfort zone. It's always going to be easier for you to do what's familiar—what you're used to. And even though that *familiar* may not be healthy, or get you to the finish line you're after, you do it because it's comfortable and you don't have to think about it or put in much effort."

"I have a great example of that," shouted a man toward the back of the room. "May I share it?"

Silvia nodded, "Of course," she said.

The short man stood as he spoke loudly so the crowd could hear. "A few weeks ago I went running with a friend. In our conversation after the run my friend said he was very careful about the shoes he wore so the cushion would protect his knees and back.

"I knew it was about time for me to get new shoes, but I hadn't wanted to spend the time to check mine out, or spend the money on new ones. That evening I took a good look at my shoes and was amazed what poor condition they were in. I had run a hole in the toe. Because I pronate, the outside of the heel was worn down. And the center tread of the ball of the shoe was nearly worn through. I might as well have been running in my socks! But I was used to it. The feel of the run was familiar.

"My son and I happened to be in the shopping mall a few days later and I stepped into the shoe store to check on the price of new running shoes. There was a terrific salesman there who set me up with the most cushiony shoes, and, being the only running shoes left in the store that were my size, I paid the price. That was a Saturday.

"The following Monday I was really excited about going out with my new shoes. I got up as I usually do, a little before 5:00 A.M., and anxiously started my run. Those new shoes had air pockets in the heels. My feet and legs weren't used to having this extra bounce, let alone full tread. So I spent more time in the air than I did putting distance behind me." Several giggled from the crowd.

"The shoes felt so different from what I was used to," continued the man, "they threw me off balance. By the time I ran my three miles, I was hobbling.

"The second day went the same way. I wanted to return the shoes and wear my old ones. Even though the new shoes, in the long run, would be healthier for me, I longed for the familiar feeling of being in control of where my feet were going!" He chuckled along with the crowd.

"That day I purposely threw the old ones in the garbage because I knew they presented too much temptation for me to return to my old ways!"

"That's great," smiled Silvia. "You have to stick with it," she said. "You have to be willing to run the risk of being uncomfortable for awhile. *You have to make the good thing feel familiar before it can feel good.* " Many in the crowd nodded agreement.

"Yea," said the man, then exclaimed, "It's taken me a couple weeks, but I'm starting to get control of my shoes!" The crowd laughed.

Silvia continued, "That's a great example. However, most life changes are bigger or take more time than just new shoes! Break the bigger challenges into pieces and pace them out. Even little, focused modifications can direct you toward your goals.

"Always remember you have the free agency of choice. You are not accountable for anyone else's mission. You are responsible to learn *who and what you are.*

"If you have not received a patriarchal blessing, do so. Read it often. Ask the Lord to bless you with the opportunities and the courage to put your life in order so you may have the peace that comes from knowing the course of life you are pursuing is pleasing to your Heavenly Father.

"Regardless of what has brought you to this point, whatever your circumstances, I promise you you *can* accomplish your mission, that the Lord will bless you with the strength you need. I testify to you that you have greater reserves than you can imagine. Never give up. Even when it is uncomfortable, set your course and lean on the Lord."

Silvia paused for a moment looking over the notes she had laid out on the table at the front of the room.

"I'll tell you what let's do," she said, "let's take a five-minute break."

Immediately some individuals stood to stretch.

"Only five minutes," she said. "We've still got quite a bit of material to cover. Go to the restroom or get a drink if you need to."

Several people stood, set their folders on their chairs, and left the room. Others appeared to relax turning to a neighbor to visit.

Stephanie left the room briefly. Returning to her seat, she overheard the blonde-haired woman sitting in front of her remarking to another, "So often I'm pulled along whether I like it or not by the scheduling needs and demands I have to fill. Sometimes I think that's a blessing; I can't think about it; I haven't the time. It hurts too much to think about it anyway."

Stephanie reflected on the woman's comment, *At some point that hurt has to be dealt with. How do you feel joy if you're too busy to be aware of what you're doing?*

The woman raised her hand. Silvia had entered the room. "Yes?" questioned Silvia.

"What if you can't change your circumstance? It is what it is. You are what you are," the woman complained.

Silvia slowly drank the glass of water earlier placed on the table for her. Then looking directly at the woman, she said, "Your attitude, your vision, makes a tremendous difference on how you see and respond to your circumstances and the outcome of your life. So many doubts and fears conspire to keep you from changing for the better.

"Sometimes the hardest part of change is believing you have the personal power to bring about that change. And sometimes you just can't see how to find a realistic starting point.

"You've got to be willing to come out of your comfort zone, even if it's a negative one, and take the risk of making life better for yourself."

Silvia turned to face the crowd. "You spend time in your mind in either your area of concern or your area of influence. The more time you spend in your area of concern, which is worrying about things you have no control over, the more you are going to feel powerless. The more time you spend in your area of influence, which is worrying, acting, or reacting to things you can have some level of control over, the more you are going to feel a sense of personal power and accountability about the choices you make. You become a catalyst for change in that environment. As you do things within your control on a daily basis, your area of influence will grow."

Again looking directly at the woman, Silvia continued, "Your view of your circumstances and your self image may or may not be reality. It may be merely what you have accepted. Many of us fool even ourselves by the role we play. But sooner or later we come to question our itinerary along the pathway to death. Sooner or later you'll want to feel important and believe that what you are doing is important—a sense of purpose, of faith in what you are doing."

Silvia looked at the crowd. "Each of you, in your own way, must come to this revelation and face the problems of living life according to the person you really are.

"Finding your reality does not come without plan or effort. Find out who you are and what you really believe. Live by what you believe and don't be swayed by what you simply have accepted of yourself.

"You are in charge of this trip you're on. Listen to the Spirit. Consciously decide on your destination and develop a road map to get you there. Believe in your ability to learn and move forward. Don't measure what you are or where you are going by looking at others or by looking at where you've been. Hold yourself accountable for the route you take.

"Pray about it. Base your values and your destination on the gospel. Read your patriarchal blessing. Learn about your personal mission. Trust that Heavenly Father has a plan for you and wants you to succeed.

"A starting place might be to focus on those specific things you wrote down earlier that would give you the greatest degree of personal fulfillment to know you have accomplished in this life. When you set goals and accomplish them, you feel more in control. Goals can provide you with a sense of purpose and a road map for your journey. A goal is an objective, a plan, something you expect to do. Having a righteous purpose invigorates your mind.

"Would someone be willing to share what they wrote down that they want to accomplish?" asked Silvia.

Stephanie looked at her notes and timidly raised her hand.

"Yes, please," said Silvia.

Stephanie said quietly, "For my children and I to have strong testimonies . . ."

"I'm sorry," interrupted Silvia. "I can't hear you. Please speak louder."

Stephanie began again in a nervous but louder voice, "I wrote down 'for my children and I to have strong testimonies of the gospel of Jesus Christ,' and 'to have us all active in the Church.'"

"Good," remarked Silvia. Pointing to Stephanie she asked, "What is your name?"

"Stephanie."

"Okay, Stephanie, from what you wrote down, what is within your area of concern and what is within your area of influence?"

Stephanie read her notes to herself then suggested, "Because I can't control their decisions and how they feel, whether my children are active in the Church and have strong testimonies would be in my area of concern. Because I can control how I feel and what I do, whether I am active in the Church and have a strong testimony is within my area of influence."

Silvia nodded her agreement. "However," she said, "your example will have great influence, so as you focus on what you presently have control over—

attending your meetings, asking your children to join you for family prayer and family home evening, offering to read scriptures together—you can positively influence the outcome for them. Your area of influence might even grow to include your children's friends, your neighbors, those you work with, etc.

"Does anyone else want to share what they wrote?" asked Silvia.

"I wrote down to have my kids know I love them," said a plump, older man. Stephanie noted she also had written down *To have my children know I love them.*

"Would that be in your area of influence?" asked Silvia.

"Well, I guess I can't **make** them feel my love," the man replied.

"But you can do things that will most likely generate the feeling of being loved." Silvia smiled and asked, "What kinds of things can you do?"

"I can tell them I love them and I can hug them," the man suggested.

"Yes, those are things you are in control of. What is your name?"

"Mark."

"Yes, Mark, those things are in your area of influence. What else can he do?" Silvia asked the crowd.

"He can listen to them," said a red-headed woman.

"He can look for things to praise them for," remarked a tall, blonde gentleman.

"Okay, you've got the idea," said Silvia. "Now since written goals are realized far more often than those that remain in thought or just verbalized, let's rewrite Mark's goal in a clear statement."

Silvia turned on the overhead projector at her side and wrote on a clear plastic sheet. The words projected on the white wall behind her:

My children know I love them because:

"Word your goal as though you have already achieved it. Be specific," Silvia explained as she continued to write:

1. I tell them I love them.

"Wherever possible, date your goal." She read aloud, "I tell them I love them," then said as she added the words to the written statement, *"at least once a day."*

Silvia continued writing:

2. I listen to them.

Looking up at the crowd she said, "Write your goal statements in as few words as possible so they can be read and reviewed quickly and easily.

"Give me some suggestions of other goal statements that fit this area of concern that are within Mark's control—that are in his area of influence."

"Perhaps Mark could make a point of looking at his children when they speak to him. I know it makes a difference to my kids when I do that," said a woman sitting on the front row.

Silvia added to the overhead sheet:

3. I look at them when they speak to me.

She nodded to another person who had raised his hand.

"What about the praise thing?"

"How shall we word that?" asked Silvia.

"I catch them doing things right and tell them so," said the man.

Silvia wrote the statement as the man said it and added: *at least once a day.* Many in the crowd nodded their agreement.

"Okay, tell me a couple more. What other things can Mark do to help realize his goal?"

"Pray for them," remarked a bearded man.

"Rephrase that," said Silvia.

"I pray for them," started the man then quickly added, "every day."

"Good. One more."

"I advise them, but let them make their own decisions and I honor those decisions," said Mark.

"Great," stated Silvia. "Each of you take a moment to write goal statements from what you earlier wrote during our exercise on dying."

Stephanie copied the goal statements from the overhead sheet onto her note paper and added:

My children and I have strong testimonies of the gospel of Jesus Christ because:

*1. I pray for God's influence each morning
and thank him each night.*

2. I attend my church meetings regularly.

*3. I prepare and present a family home
evening lesson for my family each Sunday,
or give my children the opportunity to present a lesson.*

*4. I read my scriptures each evening before I
go to bed.*

5. I attend the temple once a month.

Silvia waited several minutes then spoke, "Once you've written your goal statements, review them often, at least once a day. Rewrite them, if necessary, to clarify them and make them a way of thinking, believing, then acting. At least once a week, as you review your goals, consciously look at your behavior to see if it matches your goals. If you have established realistic, attainable goals, over time, with a consistent effort, you will attain most of them.

"Once you have your goals written, formulate a schedule on paper that dates checkpoints to achieve your goals. Allow yourself the risk to dream, plan, and stretch out of your comfort zone to become what you want. Give yourself the liberty to develop your personal power."

The warning bell rang. "We only have five minutes," said Silvia. "Does anyone have any questions?"

"What if you fail?" said the negative woman sitting on the row in front of Stephanie. "What if it doesn't work? I mean to write it on paper is one thing, but to make it happen is another."

"You are your worst critic," replied Silvia. "When you evaluate how your goals and your behavior match up, recognize the progress you've made instead of the distance still ahead. You can relax and move confidently forward if you plan, and follow that plan.

"Sometimes the route you choose to accomplish a goal doesn't move you forward. And what may be important to you today may not be so significant tomorrow. As you grow, be flexible, reevaluate what you want and how you want to get it. Write it down and act on it.

"'Do something,' said Franklin D. Roosevelt, 'and when you have done something, if it works, do it some more; and if it doesn't work, do something else.'

"We usually begin a project like this with enthusiasm, belief, and energy, but enduring to complete our goals is another matter. Too often the vision of what we can accomplish dissipates as our time and abilities are challenged.

"Believe in yourself. Start each day with a clean slate of self-expectancy. Dwell on your positive qualities and use them to your best advantage. Use your strengths to help achieve your goals. Decide to be happy and hopeful. Replace your frustration and worry with action planning. Face life with joy, interpreting opportunities and experiences with a positive sense. Most of our limits are self-imposed and don't reflect our real ability nor capacity. Reject the fear of failure and have the courage to act on your individual purpose.

> You can do as much as you think you can,
> But you'll never accomplish more;
> If you're afraid of yourself, dear friend,
> There's little for you in store,
> For failure comes from the inside first,
> It's there if we only knew it,
> And you can win, though you face the worst,
> If you feel that you are going to do it.

(Reprinted from *The Collected Verse of Edgar A. Guest,* © 1984 by Edgar A. Guest. Used with permission of NTC/Contemporary Publishing Company.)

"It's not going to be easy. Keep that fact in mind, but only as a shadow to your vision of success.

"At my last visit to the Museum of Science and Industry in Chicago," Silvia continued, "I was inspired by the work and determination prominent in one of the exhibits—a large incubator containing fertile chicken eggs and a few newly-hatched chicks.

"I stood by and watched a chick struggle as it worked its way through the shell of an egg and flop to the incubator floor in exhaustion. It lay there wet for some time, every ounce of energy spent except that for breathing. Gradually it began to move and very slowly dried. In time it stood peeping its delight to be alive and began working on another goal—to find something to eat!

"If the chick had given up its fight for freedom from the egg, it would have died. If you give up your fight to succeed, to grow, and to accomplish your goals, eventually your vision will wither and your will to do will die. Expect it to be hard, but maintain a passion to finish.

"Your doing needn't be in great leaps. Just like little chips in the egg shell eventually opened the way for the chick, little consistent accomplishments directed toward a given target will allow you to maintain belief in your ability to be successful in reaching that target.

"Break your goals into specific, achievable parts—parts that are small enough you can experience some degree of success frequently.

"The speed with which you head along your path is not as important as the direction you are going."

Stephanie raised her hand. "Yes?" asked Silvia.

"It's really frustrating when you have so little time to do those nurturing things you used to do. There's so much out of your control. I've never been a single parent before. Sometimes I make a mistake in judging what will work and what won't. I feel like I'm hanging on to a *very* skinny thread."

"Take responsibility for your actions and attitudes. Develop the habit of choosing your responses to life's experiences," responded Silvia. "Make yourself a product of your decisions instead of your conditions.

Your growth will be in direct proportion to the effort and energy you put into it.

"Invest in the tools necessary to enable you to succeed. One of the most important tools is time. Commit a given amount of consistent, concentrated time to accomplish the job well done.

Simplify the things that don't really matter, and organize yourself on paper so you gain control of your day, and pace your path to success.

"When frustration seems endless, despite your degree of effort, go back to the level where you felt successful. When you return to a level where something feels easy, you regain enthusiasm.

"People who see mistakes as opportunities for learning can keep going as challenges appear. Use mistakes as evidence that you should search for information, not that you should give up.

"Your creative abilities will grow as you recognize new avenues to achieve your ambitions. Reevaluate where you're headed and how you want to get there. Determine where you are now, what went wrong, and why. Pat yourself on the back for trying. Begin to feel a sense of satisfaction not just for those workable parts that go well and are accomplished, but for the times you tried, even if it didn't work. The trying, itself, is an accomplishment."

After a brief pause, Silvia added, "Keep your perspective—handle today what you can do today. Start slowly, pace steadily, so you can finish strongly—like the fabled turtle.

"Hang in there! Be confident in where you anchor that thin thread you're clinging to. Anchor it with the Lord. Do the best you can do; no one could ask more of you. Then expect He will fight for you. Gradually you'll see more than just a view of survival.

"A reporter asked a 64-year-old ultradistance runner how he runs a hundred miles. The runner replied, 'I don't run a hundred miles; I run one mile a hundred times.' Sometimes it works best to focus on running the mile right in front of you rather than thinking about the whole race ahead. A difficult task becomes more manageable when you direct your energy to completing that piece of the task that you face at the moment rather than wasting energy by worrying about what's to come.

"When you set goals and achieve them, you gain a sense of value and respect for yourself and you feel more in control of your life. But don't be afraid to experience the richness of the process of accomplishing those goals. Achieving the end goal is simply a by-product of developing a healthy, vibrant, resourceful lifestyle.

"The difference between a dreamer and a doer is the doer makes a plan, then acts on that plan. The doer doesn't live in the past nor in the future. She feels the exhilarating satisfaction of achieving her unique purpose by reflecting on the past, having the vision of tomorrow, and the doing of today."

The final class bell rang. The crowd began to shuffle. Silvia gathered their attention once more as she quickly concluded. "Live each day of your life as you would climb a mountain. Occasionally glance toward the summit to keep your goal in mind, but enjoy every passing moment and the many beautiful scenes you can observe from each new vantage point. Climb deliberately, steadily. Often the view from the summit will surprise you; your expectations may broaden as you reach the envisioned climax of your journey."

Chapter 5

The crowd dispersed in the hall to find various classes. Stephanie followed as far as the lobby. *I'd better write this down before I forget it,* she thought as she sat on a couch and opened the blue folder on her lap.

She quickly scanned her notes:

My children and I have strong testimonies of the gospel of Jesus Christ because:
1. *I pray for God's influence each morning and thank him each night.*
2. *I attend my church meetings regularly.*
3. *I prepare and present a family home evening lesson for my family each Sunday, or I give my children the opportunity to present a lesson.*
4. *I read my scriptures each evening before I go to bed.*
5. *I attend the temple once a month.*

My children know I love them because:
1. *I tell them I love them at least once a day.*
2. *I listen and look at them when they speak to me.*
3. *I catch them doing things right and tell them so at least once a day.*
4. *I pray for them every day.*
5. *I advise them, but let them make their own decisions and I honor those decisions.*

Then she added:

6. *I meet with each of my children one-on-one at least once a month to let them talk about how they feel.*

The bell rang signaling the beginning of the next class. Stephanie closed her folder and joined others still looking for their classrooms

In a rushed, fleeting thought she asked herself, *Where am I going to find the energy?. . . There, there's the class. 'Achieving More Balance in Your Life,'* she read from a poster on the wall. *Oh my,* she thought stopping in mid-step at the doorway. A handsome man, the instructor, stood high on a ladder just left of the classroom's center-front. He dramatically draped a rich-yellow cape about his broad shoulders.

"Hello," he said to the crowd in a deep voice. "Welcome!"

The crowd grew silent. *How can he do that?* thought Stephanie sighting a single seat on the front row. *I'd never have the nerve to do that.*

"You there," the instructor shouted as Stephanie edged her way to claim the seat. "Do you know God loves you?" the instructor asked. As she sat down, Stephanie was embarrassed to look up and realize he was talking to her. With a smile and in a pleasant voice, he answered his own question. "He does, you know. God is very much aware of you. And he won't try you beyond your ability to bear.

"Base the love you need on your relationship with Him," the instructor said to the crowd. "Get your confidence and your self esteem from your relationship with God. But remember, it's not enough to acknowledge your worth in the sight of the Lord. You've got to value yourself—to like yourself. *You've* got to matter to *you.*"

In a sweeping motion the instructor hurled the edge of the cape at his side and placed his hand on his hip. "Know who you are; have a positive focus—confident in your purpose. Then it won't matter," he paused smiling warmly, "it won't matter what others think of you. When you feel firmly rooted with the Lord, you can even stand on a rickety, tall ladder, wear an obnoxious gold cape, and have everyone stare at you." The crowd broke out in laughter.

"Lucius Seneca, a Roman statesman, author, and philosopher said, 'The most powerful is he who has himself in his own power,'" continued the instructor as he laid the cape on the top rung and climbed down the ladder.

"Many of you may question your value because your identity was seated with one individual for however long. Now that individual is no longer in your picture, whether it is because of death or because of divorce. Sometimes it's difficult to figure out who you are without them.

"In the case of divorce, it may not matter what others tell you. They may tell you you are wonderful, strong, valuable. But the hurt matters more, particularly if your previous companion didn't value you enough to be honest with you, to give you what you gave him or her, or to honor the covenants the two of you made with the Lord.

"Satan is working overtime to wipe away, to destroy, your confidence, your focus on your righteous purpose. In fact, disposing of his negative influence, consciously pushing a cancel button to negative thoughts and self talk, is essential to your growth."

The instructor intently looked at each individual in the crowd as he spoke. Moving closer to the front row, he said, "There is always going to be change. The only constant, sure thing is God's love." He looked directly at Stephanie and smiled. "Take joy in living His commandments and believe the Lord is overlooking all things for your good."

Stephanie returned his smile. She felt peace and energy around him.

"Think about yourself, talk to yourself, in positive terms," continued the instructor. "Doing so leads you to a more positive attitude toward your circumstances, experiences, and other people. As you look for the good in others and for the positive side of situations, you experience a greater sensitivity to other people's feelings and needs.

"Guard against becoming too busy. That can happen whether you have to work outside the home or not."

"How do you do that?" spontaneously questioned someone in the crowd. "Let's talk real life here. We all have certain things we have to do each day. We have pretty rigid schedules, you know. We're automatically too busy."

Stephanie could barely see the woman, but realized she was the same negative-speaking woman from the previous class.

"You do it," responded the instructor, "by eliminating the unnecessary. Yes, you may have to work to provide for your family, but many of you become 'busy' to give yourselves an excuse to not have to feel—to not deal with the reality of your life.

"You do it," repeated the instructor, "by slowing your pace, by eliminating the unnecessary 'busy,' by opening the eyes and ears of your heart to feel and experience the soft and gentle, the here and now.

"You have the same number of hours each day as people you admire who calmly accomplish great things at the same time they sensitively develop wonderful relationships. What are you exchanging for your 24 hours?

"Slacken your pace to take time to reflect on and appreciate the magnificence of God and His creations.

"Early one Saturday morning as I walked down my narrow driveway, I happened to notice the lawn. It was covered with tiny droplets of dew. Each separate drop of moisture was a little, clear ball delicately balancing at the tip of a blade of grass. I stooped down to marvel at the exquisite sight, then hurried back to the house. My youngest son was the only other person up at that time. I asked him to come outside with me. He quickly put on his shoes and joined me in the front yard. Together we spontaneously smiled and enjoyed looking and talking about one of the marvels of nature. Later, when I returned home from an errand, the dew had vanished. I realized I hadn't noticed those beautiful, individual balls like that before, yet they had been there at my feet often.

"Do you take the time to stop outside to hear the red cardinal chirping to its mate? Or do you reach your hand beyond the eaves to feel the gentleness of an early summer rain? Have you walked outside at dawn and paused long enough to look at the colors of the sky?

"This morning, the clouds over my house were a beautiful pink-mauve. As the sun emerged, the trees formed dark silhouettes in the woods against a backdrop of turquoise, gray, and yellow. Then the brightness of day revealed a brilliant blue sky smudged with powdery white clouds.

"Slow your momentum sufficiently to see the beauty around you and to enjoy the companionship of peace.

"When you're with your children, are you there just in body? Or do you hear them, see them, understand them?

"Is your daily race so swift you haven't time or energy to reach out and give or receive a hug?

"Part of maintaining balance in your life is taking time to build and bond relationships with family and friends. Work to improve your communication skills. Use more than your voice to connect. Use your eyes, ears, and heart as well. If you really look at your children when they talk to you, you can get a clearer more complete picture of the message they're trying to convey. You can sense whether they are happy, excited, hurt, embarrassed, or feeling guilty just by looking at their eyes and body language."

Stephanie repeated her goal to herself, *I listen and look at them when they speak to me.*

"The tone of the voice often says more than the words. That subject could be another workshop entirely! Did you know fifty-five percent of all understanding comes from body language? Thirty-eight percent of understanding comes from voice inflection and tone." Emphasizing each word, the instructor said, "Only seven percent comes from the content of what you say—the actual words.

"Even at that, words have a profound impact. Words are double edged swords. They can break down trust, take away power and creativity, and create hostility. *Or* they can *build* trust, *encourage* power and creativity, and *support* positive bonding.

"Humor is an important form of communication. Touch, that wonderful sense of touch, is another powerful communicator. Don't be afraid to give hugs to your children no matter how old they are. You know, you can't give a hug without receiving one! Four hugs a day for each member of the family will take friction out of the home."

Stephanie read her goal, *My children know I love them because: I tell them I love them at least once a day.* Then quickly she rewrote the last half:

> *I tell them I love them and touch them with*
> *a hug or shoulder squeeze at least once a day.*

"Purposely prioritize your time," continued the instructor, "to develop relationships with family and friends. Slow down your busyness to have time to listen, praise, forgive, and love. Purposely prioritize your time to develop a working relationship with your Heavenly Father through prayer, personal scripture study, and temple attendance. With these things in order, you will find peace.

"A couple weeks ago I attended the baptism of my niece. Several children were being baptized. My sister was the speaker. She spoke of peace saying, 'Peace is quiet happiness. It is a quiet, happy feeling. You feel peaceful when you are following God's plan.'

"Remember, *people and feelings are significantly more important than things done.* Realize you are a free agent and responsible for your role in what happens in your life. Remember who and what you are. Believe in the power and the magic within you. Dream of what you are capable of becoming. And work to make that dream a reality by being self-determined, not self-destructive. Seek for balance in your life to diminish strain, to be a more effective, positive you, and to create your happiness."

The instructor called a five-minute intermission. . . .

The class promptly reconvened.

"Now that we've discussed achieving balance in your life by taking the time to feel the soft and gentle and by developing confidence in yourself through your relationship with your Heavenly Father," began the instructor anew, "let's discuss five additional key aids to balance. But first, are there any comments on what we've already covered?"

A hand immediately popped up. "Yes?" queried the instructor.

"I've been thinking about what you said about listening and communication. And I realized that when a person speaks, what is said inevitably reflects where that person has been or, in other words, what he or she has experienced. If you listen for how *that person* is feeling and try not to compare it to what *you* are feeling or what *you* have experienced, you will have a greater chance of perceiving what his or her words are trying to convey or communicate."

"Thank you," said the instructor. Pointing to another raised hand, "Yes?" he asked.

"When we pray, we should remember the power of words. We should think and speak in specifics."

"I agree," said the instructor. "Last comment," he stated signaling a thin, dark man in the crowd.

"I have a comment regarding the peace you talked about having when you are following God's plan. If you read your patriarchal blessing often and ask the Lord to bless you with the opportunities and the courage to put your life in order, and you act on those opportunities when they happen (as surely they will), you may have the peace that comes from knowing you are following the Father's will."

"Good point," remarked the instructor.

Hastily Stephanie wrote on her note paper:

Read patriarchal blessing

"Okay, now let's discuss five additional key aids to achieving balance in your life. Any suggestions of what they might be?" the instructor asked.

"Money," shouted the negative woman across the room.

"Enough money helps, but I'm talking about keys that balance regardless of your financial situation. They are: proper eating, sleep, exercise, music, and hope.

"In the Doctrine and Covenants we learn the Lord expects us to take care of our bodies. If we do that, he will bless us. Everyone makes conscious choices in this area of daily living, but rarely do we connect these choices with the way we handle hard times. Taking care of our physical bodies makes it easier for us to think clearly, endure stress, and react positively to the adventures adversity brings.

"Your mind and body work hand in hand to make the whole. To be efficient and productive, you must be spiritually, emotionally, and physically well nourished, as well as physically rested. How you maintain your body has a tremendous bearing on your ability to fulfill your goals."

"But how do you find the time?" came a spontaneous reaction from someone in the crowd. "How do you find the time to exercise?"

Another person complained, "I'm too tired. I don't have the energy to exercise."

"Actually," responded the instructor, "as you become more fit, you'll find exercise *gives* you more energy. And regular exercise doesn't have to take more than thirty to forty minutes three to four times a week.

"Regardless of your present physical state you can do some form of exercise. By doing so you automatically feel better about yourself and your circumstance.

"Whatever exercise you choose, arrange a routine time to do it. Allow some flexibility, but have a definite plan," explained the instructor. "At different seasons of your life you will have to adjust that plan, but not the *habit.* Develop a habit to use time to move your body.

"Be patient and build your program slowly, developing a foundation of strength and fitness before extending endurance. Your love of life increases as your body becomes more fit. You feel better, look better, and have the *want* power to do better.

"Much of what you do or don't do depends on your ability to visualize yourself accomplishing it, *and* on your attitude. You have tremendous reserves. You are capable of much more than you imagine. As you build physical strength through consistent maintenance, your mental power to visualize your greater abilities will bloom. Your coping power and endurance in all matters will increase.

"Although the strength I gain from exercise is a key factor for me, the time I spend exercising is most valuable to me as my time to think, to commune with God, to look ahead and plan.

"I run," said the instructor. "In the creative action of running, I become convinced of my own importance, certain that my life has significance. Fitness probably has something to do with that. With fitness comes an awareness, a physical intelligence and sensual connection with everything around me.

"Regular exercise indicates that you have respect not only for your time, but for the time of those you impact. The amount of time spent exercising (thirty to forty minutes of aerobics, three to four times per week plus other exercises for strength, endurance and flexibility) will more than be recouped by the increased efficiency with which everything else is done.

"Listen to your body. Don't push yourself too far and risk injury. But on those days you hear yourself say, 'I'm too tired,' or, 'I don't feel like it,' learn to interpret the message. Disregard the voice of your negative self. Make the *doing* habit rule in all cases other than illness or injury.

"Don't be misled. Exercise is not a luxury. It is a *necessity.*

"Taking the time to exercise regularly is like taking out a health insurance policy. But the advantages are not just future oriented, many are immediate. You will be able to sleep better, improve regularity, reduce stress and tension, be more flexible, stronger, attractive, and self-confident. People who exercise have healthier skin. Exercise is linked to strengthening the immune system and slowing down the progress of osteoporosis. Also, aerobic exercise will lead to a moderation in your appetite. And a consistent, moderate workout can make you look and feel sexier," smiled the instructor.

"You have to have strength before you can use it, and I've found that the more I develop within myself, the more I have to give to others.

"Keeping yourself well nourished should be a priority. The result is stronger relationships. And taking responsibility for your own well-being releases your family from the burden of trying to keep you on an even keel.

"To feel God's love, value yourself enough to become your own willing caretaker.

"Let's move on to the next key aid—music."

Again Stephanie quickly added to her notes:

Exercise

"I'm not talking about just any music," the instructor suggested. "I'm talking about music that helps you feel the Lord by your side.

"Songs, music, can greatly influence your thoughts. Appropriate music is a tool of our Heavenly Father. Elder Boyd K. Packer said, 'We are able to feel and learn very quickly through music . . . some spiritual things that we would otherwise learn very slowly' ("The Arts and the Spirit of the Lord," *Ensign,* Aug. 1976, p. 61).

"Being selective about what you listen to can have a definite bearing on your attitude. Select songs with messages that inspire faith in a loving Heavenly Father and promote love toward your family and friends—sometimes it's the actual words of a song, sometimes it's the melody, sometimes it is the beautiful memories of when or how it was sung.

"Music alone can put a smile on my face, make me feel cheerful and happy. Music can make me feel like I can face my challenges with determination and accomplish what needs to be done. It can invigorate me, make me feel strong, excited, awake, and alive.

"Music can create for me a reverent atmosphere as well. There is great power in music. The sound of a fall breeze shuffling leaves can be music to my ears—even the silent 'sound' of large, fluffy snowflakes falling to the ground. . . ."

After a short pause, the instructor continued, "The last aid is hope. Never abandon hope. Faith and hope provide you with the power and the will to do.

"I cannot over emphasize how important it is to believe in yourself, in your ability to learn and move forward. It is important to know you can maintain loving relationships and that you can have personal control or power in your life. Hope, belief, or faith are powerful enough to release hormones in the brain called endorphins. Endorphins magnify your energy, drive, and alertness and increase your positive vision of life.

"Habits allow you to do several things at the same time. Most habits are good, but when you drastically change your life, old habits that worked in your previous environment may not work in your new environment or with your new experiences.

"Your attitudes are subconscious habits. If you want to change your life, look at your attitudes about yourself, about others, or about situations that may be holding you back, and consciously decide to change those attitudes."

The instructor climbed back up the ladder and put on the cape. He swirled the edge of the cape around him like a cocoon. "I have chosen gold for my cape," he explained, "because through countless ages, gold has been a symbol of loyalty. We must each envelop ourselves in loyalty to the Lord, loyalty to the covenants and promises we make. This will determine what we are in the sight of God.

"I believe there is yet a great deal each of you are supposed to accomplish in this life. You each are free agents. You determine your eternal condition by the choices and effort you make. You must be doers and not just hearers. As you are put in positions to have your loyalty tested, again by your personal choices you are proven.

"Do not worry about being a success in your mission. The Lord has sent you to earth to fulfill that mission. He created you to be a king or a queen. He will provide a way for you to accomplish the work.

"Never turn away from what you believe in your heart to be right. And lean on the arm of God to determine those beliefs.

"My daughter gave me a great quote last night," continued the instructor. "It is by Brent A. Barlow. 'What we are is more important than what we have been. And what we can become is more important than what we are.'

"You all greatly underestimate your worth and your potential. It is time for you to seek for the highest that is in you, to be strong by gaining knowledge through study and prayer, to have hope, believe, faith that the Lord will deliver you, and to move with confidence and power in loyalty to God.

"He does not ask more than you can bear. He prepares the way before you. I bear you this testimony in the name of Jesus Christ. Amen."

R i n g, blared the final class bell. Stephanie hadn't even heard the warning bell. Quietly the crowd rose one by one. Many went to the front of the room to thank the instructor as he descended from the ladder. All eventually collected in the chapel with other workshop participants to hear the keynote speaker, the stake president. The benches were lined with miniature paper backpacks. Stephanie opened her little backpack to find colorful sheets of paper.

"I know this has been a long morning for most of you," began the stake president, "some of you weren't able to attend as many workshops as you'd like. But all of you will agree, I'm sure, that you have benefited from the instruction and discussions today." The participants of the crowd appeared as small waves nodding in agreement.

"On the bench there should be a paper backpack for each of you. Take out the pencil and papers. Use the two large white papers to make a written list of all the things you feel are burdening you. Please do that now."

After a long pause, the stake president continued, "Tear the list into strips (each separate item burdening you on a separate strip). Now put all the white strips of paper in your backpack. Imagine each strip is wrapped around a heavy rock. Feel the weight of the pack? This is what you carry. These are the things you worry about, that weight you down, that keep you from feeling joy.

"One by one take the strips out of your backpack. Read and analyze each one to determine if someone can help you with that burden, or even if it's your responsibility to carry at all. The objective is to own what is actually yours, to give away what really belongs to others, and to allow others to carry their share where team effort is appropriate.

"As you analyze each item you've written on your white strips of paper, on the small, green sheets rewrite those items that are your responsibility—that you should own. The little, yellow sheets of paper are for you to use to rewrite those items you can cautiously, tactfully give away to others. On red, rewrite all items you can get rid of."

The stake president waited while the participants wrote and evaluated. Then he added, "Now, prioritize those items you must carry—those you've written onto your green papers. Which ones can or should you do something about today? Make a mental plan of what piece you can do and when. . . . Put only the green sheets back in your pack. Feel how much lighter the pack is?

"You know, in my role as stake president, I have met with most of you. I recognize your great faith, your skill, your desires to please your Heavenly Father—to be worthy. As you carry and work through your burdens, I trust that Heavenly Father will guide, lead, and direct you, that He will bless you with joy and the sweet desires of your heart fulfilled.

"Remember to meet what appears to be defeat with resiliency. What might seem to be a terrible failure can be something that leads you to a great opportunity. Don't curse the darkness. Be the one to light a candle!

"I'd like you to pay attention to the fourth verse of the closing song. Whenever you find yourself weighted down, feeling taken for granted, not progressing, or lonely, apply the fourth verse of this song. Avoid feeling sorry for yourself in whatever transitional stage you are now in. Accept my challenge to develop an immovable personal testimony of the gospel of Jesus Christ and lose yourself in service to your fellowmen.

"You are loved unconditionally. To find the happiness you are searching for, love in return, and give what you can give.

"Allow your Heavenly Father to be your coach. And hang in there with a strong cord of conviction and total commitment to the vision of becoming a champion. . . ."

I feel my Savior's love. . . .
His Spirit warms my soul. . . .
I feel my Savior's love;
Its gentleness enfolds me. . . .
I feel my Savior's love
And know that he will bless me. . . .
I'll share my Savior's love
By serving others freely.
In serving I am blessed.
In giving I receive.
He knows I will follow him,
Give all my life to him.
I feel my Savior's love,
The love he freely gives me.

("I Feel My Savior's Love," *Children's Songbook,* pp.74–75. Used by permission, © 1979 by Sonos Music Resouces, Inc.)

Chapter 6

When the single woman arrived home, she found her three children lounging in the small front room. In their TV-hypnotic state, they seemed oblivious of her return.

Stephanie was relieved to find them safe but overcome afresh by the loneliness of her heavy load. She looked at the dust on the furniture and remembered the laundry was not done. She slowly walked to the kitchen and viewed the dirty dishes haphazardly filling the sink, a pan on the stove, and open cereal boxes and milk still sitting on the countertop. Feeling the warmth of the milk container, she leaned with disappointment to determine its souring smell. *It will have to be used in cooking. It can't be just wasted,* she thought as she screwed on the cap and removed the container to the refrigerator.

It isn't fair. I can't go anywhere or do anything fun without the work doubling. I shouldn't have gone to the conference. Immediately she pictured a large, red cancel button labeled with the instructor's words, "Push to stop negative thoughts and self talk."

That kind of negative talk will get me nowhere. This is my mountain. I've got to face it. I've got to do it.

She went upstairs to her bedroom to change her clothes and take a quiet minute to become aware of her options and how she might choose a better way.

Stephanie knelt at her bedside. "Dear Heavenly Father," she pleaded, "please help me to be good. How do I pull it together? How do I make it work? I can't do it all. . . ." Closing her prayer, she opened her wet eyes and looked at the conference note folder and small, paper backpack she'd placed on the bed. A corner of her yellow sheet used in the stake president's message peeked from the top of the backpack.

"Those are the items you can cautiously, tactfully give away to others," she remembered him saying. She pulled the little sheet from the pack and sat on the bed to review it. On the yellow paper she had written:

> *Laundry, clean bathroom, dishes, fix meals, lawn care, floors, and dusting*

"Allow others to carry their share where team effort is appropriate," the stake president had said.

Okay, Stephanie exclaimed to herself, *we need to become a team.*

Reentering the front room, on her way to the television control, Stephanie purposely walked by each of her children to gently touch their knee, arm, or shoulder.

"Hey, Mom, what are you doing?" asked Cheri, Stephanie's oldest daughter. "We're in the middle of a program. Turn it back on."

Stephanie smiled and pulled a chair to sit on in front of the television.

"No," grumbled Eric, Stephanie's scout.

"M - o - m," complained Alison, the youngest family member.

"The conference was wonderful," Stephanie began. "You would have enjoyed seeing one of the instructors wearing a gold cape standing high on a tall ladder!

"It's hard for me to come home, though, and realize I've still got to do everything just like I had a full day's worth of time ahead of me. I need your help.

"Silvia, another instructor, said to break your challenges into pieces and then work on those pieces. It's hard for me to be happy when I feel I'm alone carrying the load for our family. If each of you would be responsible for one or more of those pieces, we could have more fun together, I could feel like smiling more, and you'd each feel good because you'd be doing your share.

"We can accomplish everything that needs to be done if we act as a team and invite our Heavenly Father to be a part of that team. Will you help me?"

"I can dust the furniture," suggested Alison, "and make my bed and clean my room."

"I guess I could take care of the yard," offered Eric.

"I'd be willing to do my own laundry," stated Cheri.

"That's great," exclaimed Stephanie. "Could you take turns cleaning the bathroom and vacuuming the house? How about the meals? We all have to eat. How about everyone taking a turn to be in charge of fixing dinner once a week?"

"But I don't know how to cook," whined Alison.

"You know how to make sandwiches, don't you?" stated Stephanie.

"Yea," Alison reluctantly responded with a half-smile.

"Ali, I can teach you how to make pancakes," offered Cheri.

"But that's a breakfast food," said Eric.

"Who says it has to be only for breakfast?" interrupted Stephanie. "That's great Cheri. Alison, how about you fix Monday dinners? Eric do you want Tuesdays or Wednesdays?"

"Wednesdays I have scouts, Mom, and I've got soccer on Tuesdays."

"Oh, yea, how about Thursdays then?" asked Stephanie.

"Okay," agreed Eric. "I'll do the yard work and straighten my room on Saturdays. Okay?"

"Great."

"I guess I could do the dinners on Tuesdays," said Cheri.

"Thank you, Cheri. Now, who will clean the bathroom this week?" asked Stephanie. She knodded to Alison's raised hand.

"I'll make a chart showing who's turn it is to do what each week. Okay?" asked Cheri.

"That would be wonderful," Stephanie smiled. "Thank you."

Thank you Heavenly Father. Thank you for your help, she thought as the children separated happily to carry their piece of the workload and the single woman went to clean the kitchen and fix dinner.

Within a couple hours the house was straightened and they had eaten and cleaned up after dinner. With a large bowl of popcorn, Stephanie and her children quietly relaxed together watching a magic show on television. Before going to bed they knelt, as usual, for family prayer. It was Alison's turn to pray.

"Thank you, Heavenly Father, for my family. Thank you for the fun we had tonight. Please bless Mom and Cheri and Eric and me. Please help us to be safe. . . ."

Alone in her bedroom the single woman opened her note folder again to review her goals.

> *My children and I have strong testimonies of the gospel of Jesus Christ because:*
> *1. I pray for God's influence each morning and thank him each night.*

I need to remember to say my prayer in the morning, she thought.

> *2. I attend my church meetings regularly.*
> *3. I prepare and present a family home evening lesson for my family each Sunday, or I give my children the opportunity to present a lesson.*

Tomorrow we'll have a lesson. Let's see, thought Stephanie, *maybe we'd better have a lesson on putting the milk away!* She chuckled to herself.

> *4. I read my scriptures each evening before I go to bed.*
> *5. I attend the temple once a month.*
>
> *My children know I love them because:*
> *1. I tell them I love them and touch them with a hug or shoulder squeeze at least once a day.*

Stephanie set the folder down on the bed, walked to the girls' bedroom and knocked on the closed door. "Come in," they chimed.

Opening the door, Stephanie said, "I love you both girls. Thank you for your help tonight."

"Love you too, Mom," responded the girls.

Stephanie turned to Eric's room, the door open, and said, "Eric, I love you."

"You too, Mom," Eric smiled.

Alone again in her room, Stephanie continued to review her notes.

> *2. I listen and look at them when they speak to me.*
> *3. I catch them doing things right and tell them so at least once a day.*
> *4. I pray for them every day.*
> *5. I advise them, but let them make their own decisions and I honor those decisions.*
> *6. I meet with each of my children one-on-one at least once a month to let them talk about how they feel.*

We always have family prayer too, thought Stephanie as she rewrote the fourth goal.

> *4. We have family prayer together every night; every day in my personal prayers, I ask Heavenly Father to bless each of my children.*

She read her brief additional notes:

> *Read patriarchal blessing* and *exercise*

I'll find my patriarchal blessing tomorrow after church. I can't afford any exercise equipment but I guess I could walk each day. . . .

Hmm, how shall I write it? she asked herself.

> *I keep myself in good physical condition by walking each day.*

No, thought Stephanie, *I'd better not push that on Sunday.*

> *I keep myself in good physical condition by walking at least six days a week.*

Stephanie set her goal sheets on the lamp stand beside her bed and picked up her scriptures to read. The black, ribbon marker was at Mosiah chapter 18. She began reading about Alma preaching to the people and organizing the Church of Christ. *That's us. That's how we need to be,* thought Stephanie as she reread verse 21.

> And he commanded them that there should
> be no contention one with another, but that
> they should look forward with one eye, having
> one faith and one baptism, having their hearts
> knit together in unity and in love one towards
> another.

Please, Heavenly Father, she thought, *please help me and my children to be "knit together in unity and love." And please help us to eliminate contention. . . .*

Sunday morning Stephanie and her children attended church. After lunch she reread her goals remembering what Silvia had said at the conference: "Once you've written your goal statements, review them often, at least once a day. Rewrite them, if necessary, to clarify them and make them a way of thinking, believing, then acting. At least once a week, as you review your goals, consciously look at your behavior to see if it matches your goals."

Gotta have a family home evening lesson today, read my patriarchal blessing, and work on the exercise thing, Stephanie thought. She pulled the family home evening manual from the bookshelf and looked in the index for a lesson on finances and budgeting. The only listing referred to a brief message on financial security needed in marriage.

> Brethren and sisters, plan and work in a
> way that will permit you to be happy even as
> you do without certain things that in times of
> affluence may have been available to you. Live
> within your means and not beyond them.

Where you have a plot of land, however small, plant a garden. Staying close to the soil is good for the soul. Purchase your essentials wisely and carefully. Strive to save a portion of that which you earn. Do not mistake many wants for basic needs.

Teach your children these basic principles in your family councils.

(Spencer W. Kimball, in "Conference Report," April 1981, pp. 107–8; or "Ensign," May 1981, p. 80.) [*Family Home Evening Resource Book*, p. 136.]

I remember Mom's box, Stephanie reflected. *My mom and dad were always so careful with money.* She couldn't think of where she could find a box like her mother's but thought of another option. She collected the necessary aids and then gathered her family at the kitchen table for the lesson.

"Who would like to choose a song and lead the singing?" asked Stephanie.

"I would," responded Ali. "Let's sing 'Love One Another.'"

Stephanie helped Alison begin with the right note. "As I have loved you . . ."

"Eric, since you're the priesthood holder in our home, will you call on someone to give the opening prayer?" asked Stephanie.

"Cheri," Eric said knodding his head as a request.

After the amen, Stephanie placed a small, open, corrugated box at the center of the table. "When I was growing up, my dad, your grandpa, gave to my mom just the right number of one-dollar bills, five-dollar bills, and ten-dollar bills to make up the amount of money they had budgeted to cover those things my mother was responsible to pay for during the week. She had a box like this one," Stephanie pointed to the brown box, "only a little bigger. Inside the box were small cardboard compartments labeled 'House,' 'Food,' 'Clothing,' and so on. My mother placed the bills in each compartment according to the amount she and my father had agreed to spend.

"I remember, as a young girl, needing a new pair of shoes. I went to my mother and asked, 'Can I have a new pair of shoes this week?'

"My mother said, 'Let's see if we have enough money.' She took me into her bedroom, opened the cupboard, and pulled out the box. Together we counted the money that was in the clothing compartment. There wasn't enough for a new pair of shoes. My mother smiled and said, 'We'll get them for you, but you'll just have to wait until we have enough money in the box.'

"A week or so later there was enough money and I got my new shoes but, you see, I learned to wait and plan; I learned to budget.

"We need to do the same thing," Stephanie continued. "I want you to know what's happening with our money. I don't want you to think I'm just neglecting to get something for you that you need. I am going to make up a budget for us.

"You know I earn very little. Your father left us with a lot of bills and no money, and we cannot depend on him to pay for your support as he should. Too many times he has failed to give us the money.

"I don't have a box like my mother's but we can use envelopes." Stephanie spread letter-sized envelopes out on the table. I'll label each envelope, and when I get my pay check on Wednesday, I'll go to the bank and have them cash it into the right number of bills for what we budget.

"I remember my dad had a notebook where he accounted for all his income and expenses. I'm going to write or list our budget in this notebook." Stephanie showed the children a green loose-leaf notebook. "Since I want you to know where we stand, I'll keep this book on the bookshelf in the front room. You can look at it when you want to.

"This is a quote from Spencer W. Kimball." Stephanie read the quote from the family home evening manual.

"In the spring we need to plant a couple tomato bushes by the back patio," Cheri suggested.

Stephanie agreed then continued, "Please put the food away after you eat. We can't afford to waste what we have.

"I'll work on this budget this afternoon.

"Remember the story of the young warriors in the book of Alma?" Opening her scriptures and pointing to Alma chapter 53, Stephanie asked, "Eric would you read verses 20 through 22?"

And they were all young men, and they were exceedingly valiant for courage, and also for strength and activity; but behold, this was not all—they were men who were true at all times in whatsoever thing they were entrusted.

Yea, they were men of truth and soberness, for they had been taught to keep the commandments of God and to walk uprightly before him.

And now it came to pass that Helaman did march at the head of his two thousand stripling soldiers, to the support of the people in the borders of the land on the south by the west sea.

"What happened to these young men?" Stephanie asked.

"They had faith and were saved," responded Cheri.

"That's right. Cheri, read Alma 56:47."

Eric handed the scriptures to Cheri.

"Now they never had fought, yet they did not fear death; and they did think more upon the liberty of their fathers than they did upon their lives; yea, they had been taught by their mothers, that if they did not doubt, God would deliver them."

"Ali, will you read Alma 57:21?"

"Sure." Alison took the scriptures as Cheri offered them.

"Yea, and they did obey and observe to perform every work and command with exactness; yea, and even according to their faith it was done unto them; and I did remember the words which they said unto me that their mothers had taught them."

"Thanks," said Stephanie. "Now here," she reached for the scriptures, "in Alma chapter 58 it says:

> And those sons of the people of Ammon, of whom I have so highly spoken, are with me in the city of Manti; and the Lord has supported them, yea, and kept them from falling by the sword, insomuch that even one soul has not been slain.
>
> But behold, they have received many wounds; nevertheless they stand fast in that liberty wherewith God has made them free; and they are strict to remember the Lord their God from day to day; yea, they do observe to keep his statutes, and his judgments, and his commandments continually; and their faith is strong in the prophecies concerning that which is to come. (Alma 58:39–40.)

"You see, they could depend in full faith on the Lord protecting and preserving them because they were steadfast in their commitment and trust in Him. They trusted Him to keep His promises. Without wavering, to the core, they had a relationship with Heavenly Father.

"We can make it through our hard times too. If we obey the commandments and have faith, our Heavenly Father will help us.

"Eric, who should give the closing prayer? Oh, and who will give the lesson next week?"

Eric said, "I'll give the prayer."

"Will you give the lesson?" Stephanie asked Cheri.

"Okay," Cheri answered reluctantly. Stephanie handed her the family home evening manual.

Eric said the prayer.

That afternoon, Stephanie developed a budget on paper. It was a struggle to spread her meager income to cover the rent, utilities, food, and clothing. She realized she needed to build a cushion for car repairs and have a savings as President Kimball had counseled. It turned out to be only $5 a month for each, but it was a start. She planned $3 for entertainment. At least they could rent a video tape once a month.

Stephanie counted the money in her purse. There was just over $20. She took $10 and placed it in the envelope labeled food and left the remaining money in her purse for fuel for the car. *Let's see, the rent isn't due until Thursday. We're supposed to get a child support check on Tuesday and my paycheck on Wednesday. We'll be okay.*

Oh no, thought Stephanie, *I forgot to give the bishop my tithing. I'll have to give it to him next Sunday.* She put the prepared tithing envelope in the front pocket of her scriptures where she'd be sure to see it when she got to church.

Monday morning Stephanie got up fifteen minutes early so she could keep her promise to herself to walk. It was late fall. The yellow-leafed branches of the willow trees hung limply to the ground. The brisk air tingled the skin on her cheeks and nose.

In her mind, she heard the instructor from the conference speaking, "Do you take the time to stop outside to hear the red cardinal chirping to its mate?" Stephanie paused to hear the faint rustling of the yellow leaves.

"Or do you reach your hand beyond the eaves to feel the gentleness of an early summer rain?" Walking through the corner vacant lot, she reached her hands out on both sides to feel the tips of the waist-high, tall grasses.

"Have you walked outside at dawn and paused long enough to look at the colors of the sky?" Stephanie stood still, now back in her front yard. She leaned her head back and for a moment watched the feathered clouds swiftly move across the morning, blue sky. The earth seemed to speak a language of its own. Somehow just being outside away from her own world where worries surrounded her, she felt more aware of the sweetness of life and closer to her Heavenly Father. *Thirty minutes tomorrow,* thought Stephanie, committing to treat herself to this kindness thirty minutes a day.

Then looking down, she leaned to pick up a penny and a dirty nickel from the gray-paved sidewalk at her feet. *Every little bit helps,* she said to herself. *Oh, I wish I didn't have to worry so much about money.* And there it was, the jagged cliffs of her mountain glaring her in the face once again. . . .

Tuesday passed without a child support check; Wednesday morning Stephanie was greeted at work with the startling announcement that the home-office computer had crashed. It would take several days to input the payroll information again. Checks would not be issued for another week.

At home that evening, Stephanie surveyed the kitchen cupboards to determine what they could eat that would get them by until she received her pay check. Too many months of just making it one pay check to the next left no surplus on the shelves. She removed the last pound of meat from the freezer and a nearly empty bag of rice from the cupboard by the stove. There was a can of peas, which they would eat for dinner, and a can of corn, and two cans of tuna. There was just enough cereal and milk to get them through breakfast Thursday, a bag of pinto beans, a loaf of bread, a few eggs, and some flour and yeast. That was it. *It'll just have to stretch,* thought Stephanie. *Somehow it'll just have to stretch.*

By bedtime she was too drained and tired to read a chapter in her scriptures as she had been doing each night. *But I promised myself,* thought Stephanie. She pulled out her goal sheet, folded as a marker in her scriptures, and set the black-bound book on the bed beside her. *One verse. I've got to read at least one verse.* She unfolded the goal sheet and rewrote the fourth goal, adding just a few words.

> *4. I read **at least one verse** from the scriptures each evening before I go to bed.*

Then she randomly opened her scriptures. They fell open to the commandments of Alma to his son— Alma 38. Verse five caught her eye because it was highlighted from previous readings:

And now my son, Shiblon, I would that ye should remember, that as much as ye shall put your trust in God even so much ye shall be delivered out of your trials, and your troubles, and your afflictions, and ye shall be lifted up at the last day.

Thursday morning Stephanie told each of her children she loved them as they left the house to meet the school bus and the car pool rides. During her morning walk, she thought how grateful she was that she had already paid for a week's worth of lunch tickets for the children.

She made a tuna sandwich to take to work for her own lunch—spreading the tuna fish real thin. She took five dollars from the food envelope to buy a gallon of milk and a box of cereal on her way home from work.

The work day seemed in slow motion. Stephanie welcomed it's close. At the grocery store, she was eight cents short to buy the milk and cereal. A kind woman waiting in the checkout line behind her read Stephanie's bewildered look at the cashier and offered the additional change. Embarrassed but grateful, Stephanie thanked the woman and etched her way home.

It was Eric's night to fix dinner. Stephanie showed him how to make egg noodles and a white sauce. They coupled the noodles and sauce with their last can of tuna fish to make a tasty tuna-noodle casserole served with canned corn.

While the children did their homework, Stephanie called the landlord to ask for a reprieve until the late pay day. The landlord was not very understanding and insisted on charging a late fee if the rent was not paid on time.

"Please," pleaded Stephanie. "I'll pay you as soon as I am paid. I've never been late with the rent before. Do you see I'm not late on purpose? My work is late paying me. I'll pay you even before I buy the groceries. Please don't charge the late fee."

"All right for this one time," said the landlord. "See that I'm paid by next week. If this happens again, I'll definitely charge the fee."

Family prayer was the one sweet part of the day. Ali tenderly thanked Heavenly Father for a good place to live and for food to eat. "And thank you, Heavenly Father, for my wonderful family and that Mom knows how to make noodles."

Stephanie could hear the whisper of chuckles from Alison's siblings. "Thank you, Ali," she said smiling as she gathered her giggling, little family in a group hug.

As everyone readied for bed, Stephanie pulled the box of money envelopes from the cupboard shelf in her bedroom. She knew full well there were only five dollars in the box, but she couldn't help but thumb through the little stack and fantasize of ample cash for rent, clothes, car, and fun. *How would it be?* she queried herself sarcastically. *If only he'd pay his share. If only the child support checks would come . . .*

Retrieving the envelope labeled "Food," Stephanie returned to reality as she removed the five-dollar bill. At the conference, the stake president had said to lighten your backpack by getting rid of unrealistic expectations, seeing things as they really are, then acting on what you see.

Stephanie thought of the little red paper from the stake president's demonstration. She had written:

Do not expect money for child support.

She knelt by her bed, still rubbing the five-dollar bill between her thumb and fingers. She closed her eyes and said, "Heavenly Father, please help me to forgive him. Please help me to be able to carry the weight of my burdens like you helped the Nephites in the Book of Mormon. Please give me wisdom to know how to make it all work. . . ."

Friday morning Stephanie used the last of the tuna mixture to make herself a sandwich for lunch. Another slow work day ended with a verbal promise that pay checks would definitely be passed out the next Tuesday.

Again she stopped at the store on her way home. This time she carefully included taxes in her estimate to be sure the five dollars would cover the pound of hamburger and small package of rice she carried to the check out.

After dinner she removed and opened the bag of pinto beans from the cupboard shelf. She washed the beans, then set them in a pan of water on the kitchen counter so the beans could soak through the night. There was nothing of real substance left to eat but the beans.

Although she smiled and cheerfully interacted with the children, the invisible backpack Stephanie carried throughout the evening seemed loaded with cement blocks.

She welcomed bedtime, immediately releasing a dam of tears as she knelt at her bedside. "Oh Father, how will we make it? Why must we struggle? I have been obedient." She wanted to let out the loud sobs she felt swollen in her chest, but didn't dare let the children hear. Catching her breath, quietly she cried, "Please Father, I can't take any more. You promised you wouldn't ask any more than we could bear. You know I've reached my limit. Please send help."

Though her prayer was ended, she stayed on her knees and reached for her scriptures placed on her pillow as a reminder of her commitment to read each night. She placed her hand on the black-bound book, patting it with her fingers spread apart. *You promised. Please keep your promise,* she pleaded in her thoughts.

As she lifted her hand, she noticed the tithing envelope she had placed in the pocket of the scripture cover earlier in the week. *I could buy some fresh fruit for the children and enough food to see us through until the pay check comes. I could pay the tithing next week,* her silent tears wetting the gray envelope. *But it's not mine,* she thought. *I've always paid my tithing.*

Again Stephanie closed her eyes to beg from her unseen friend. "Oh Father, I'm so afraid. What would ye have me do?"

A thought came to her mind, *Where faith is, you don't doubt the outcome. The Lord will keep his promises.*

Stephanie sat on the edge of her bed, the black-bound book on her lap. She thought of Oma and wondered if she had faced this kind of challenge. Had she known this kind of fear? Then she recalled the scripture that she and Oma had read together about God not giving us the spirit of fear. She opened the book to 2 Tim 1:7, still marked by the wrinkled paper Oma had handed her as she left that day. She read aloud. "For God hath not given us the spirit of fear, but of power, and of love, and of a sound mind."

She remembered Oma saying, "Cling onto the words *power, love,* and *a sound mind.*"

Stephanie sat, quietly starring at the verse as the answer came to her. She read the scripture again. *And of trust,* she thought, *I guess He gives us trust if we rely on the Spirit. I've got to trust that the money will be there, that there will be a way to feed my family.* She pulled the folded goal sheet from the front of her scriptures and wrote:

I pay my tithing.

"Knock, knock," came a gentle sound on her bedroom door.

"Come in," said Stephanie.

"I heard you crying, Mom," Cheri said softly as she cautiously opened the door and stepped to Stephanie's bedside. "Are you okay?"

"Yes. I'll be fine." Stephanie replied, wiping her eyes with her hand.

Cheri sat beside her, reaching over the scriptures to give her mother a warm, sustained hug. "Remember Helaman's soldiers, Mom? I know you're worried about the money. We'll make it, just like they did. This is just a wound.

"Mom," she said sweetly, "we're going to make it through this." Cheri opened her closed fist to hand Stephanie her baby-sitting money. "This will help a little," she said.

"Oh, we can't use your money. You were going to buy a new blouse this week."

"I'll buy a new blouse another time."

What an unexpected answer to prayer, thought Stephanie. "I'm sorry Cheri," she said returning the hug.

"It's okay Mom. I don't mind. Really I don't. Remember, we're supposed to be a team."

Stephanie cradled Cheri's face in her hands and looked directly into her eyes. "Thank you sweetheart."

They hugged again. Then Cheri, smiling, left to her room. Stephanie placed the money on top of her scriptures on the bookshelf, turned out the light, and knelt once again at her bedside. "Father," she cried, "thank you. Thank you for a tender, sweet daughter. Please bless me to be wise. May I have the gift and power of the Holy Ghost to bless me to know what to do to wisely use this money. Thank you." She closed her prayer, then lay on her bed starring out the window at the yellow moon framed by the clouds as she thought, *Please bless each of my children. Thank you. Thank you for them. Please help me to know what to do to help myself and how to recognize the opportunities you make available for us.*

Everyone slept in Saturday morning. Then Cheri taught Ali how to make pancakes while Stephanie used the last of the eggs and flour to make some bread for lunch to accompany the beans she was cooking on the stove.

At the breakfast table, Stephanie thanked Cheri again. "Thank you Cheri for giving us your baby-sitting money. When we get the kitchen cleaned up, let's all go to the store to buy some milk and fruit. You can pick out your own, like an apple for today and an orange for tomorrow. Let me give you your school lunch money first so we can be sure you have that." Stephanie gave each of the children an envelope with enough money enclosed to cover their individual lunch tickets for the coming week.

Everyone enjoyed the store excursion. Eric immediately chose green apples; Cheri got a banana and an orange; Stephanie got two oranges. Ali, however, had a hard time deciding what she wanted, but finally settled on a banana and a tomato. Cheri smiled when the store clerk handed Stephanie a dollar's worth of change at the check out. Stephanie put the money in her coat pocket.

The events of the whole day seemed to be cheerful. The children cooperated in doing their share to clean, and the evening, family-centered movie on the television ended the day peacefully.

Sunday began with Stephanie kneeling at her bedside thanking Heavenly Father for her children, Cheri's generosity, and the odd peace she felt that all would be well. "Please help me to live so I can feel the Spirit. I will pay my tithing today. Please help us to stretch the bread and beans until pay day."

She no longer felt like a committee of one designated to make it all work for the family. She felt the support, the unity, of her children as a team with Heavenly Father as their coach, guide, and comforter.

Some hours later, the topic in sacrament meeting was charity. "When I give away some of my money or my time," the confident speaker said, "I have chosen to not be afraid and to trust I will always have enough to share with others."

The speaker added, "I love the feeling when I decide that I am not going to be afraid."

Stephanie reached her hand into the pocket of her coat. The change was still there from the grocery trip the night before. As she quietly felt the coins, she remembered a small child attending Cheri's birthday party years ago who had brought the gift of a slice of bread in a paper sack. Her meager means had not kept her from participating.

Stephanie gently nudged Cheri with her elbow, removed the coins from her pocket and whispered, "Do you feel okay about paying this money as fast offerings?"

"That's all we have, Mom."

"Yea, I know. But maybe there are others who have less."

Cheri nodded a reluctant "yes" and Stephanie opened the tithing envelope to add the coins and mark "fast offerings" on the receipt.

"We must have faith enough to expect the Lord will take care of what we cannot if we have done everything we can," the speaker said. "Turn to the twelfth chapter of Ether in the Book of Mormon, verse six. 'And now, I, Moroni, would speak somewhat concerning these things; I would show unto the world that faith is things which are hoped for and not seen; wherefore, dispute not because ye see not, for ye receive no witness until after the trial of your faith.'

"Heavenly Father keeps His promises. You can count on it. . . ."

At the close of the meeting, Stephanie worked her way to the front of the chapel and handed the bishop her tithing/fast offering envelope.

"How are you doing?" he asked.

"We will be fine," she answered assuredly.

All day Stephanie felt warm—a good warm, the kind you feel when you and your world are at peace. As evening approached, Stephanie remembered she had failed to read her patriarchal blessing the week before. She found it tucked into the pocket of her scripture cover. *It must have been hidden behind the tithing envelope,* she thought.

Her patriarchal blessing mentioned several things she was to do with a companion. *Hmm,* she thought, *I wonder what it would be like to have a companion like that . . .* Her thoughts were interrupted by the telephone.

"Hello," she said.

"Hi Stephanie. This is Maggie." Maggie was the ward Relief Society president. "You've been on my mind lately and I thought I'd call and just see how you're doing."

Stephanie paused. "Thanks Maggie. I think we're going to be okay. We've had kind of a rough week," she explained, "but I'm sure things are going to look up."

During their brief visit, Stephanie sensed Maggie's caring concern. Stephanie heard the bell from the front door. In a moment Eric was at her side pulling Stephanie by the hand.

"Mom, come here. You've got to see this."

"Thank you Maggie. Your call means a lot to me. Someone's at the door though, so I've got to go."

"Let me know if there's something I can do to help," said Maggie.

By this time, Cheri and Ali were standing by Eric shielding the doorway, the front door open. Their Cheshire-cat smiles seemed peculiar to Stephanie.

"Okay, what's going on here?" she said as she walked up to them.

"Ta da," they chimed as they parted like a curtain and pointed at the doorstep.

"What?" exclaimed Stephanie.

"The bell rang, and when I opened the door, this was here," Eric laughed.

Stephanie reached down to pick up a large, wheat-colored, woven basket filled with groceries: ham, stuffing mix, potatoes, canned vegetables, bread, and fruit. Eric and Cheri each picked up a brown, paper sack also filled with groceries.

The basket was labeled with a little, paper heart attached to the handle by a red, satin ribbon. A message was written on the heart: "We heard you needed some help. We hope this food will fill your stomachs and your spirits." The note was signed, "Your neighbors."

"Oh - h - h, oh my," Stephanie said in a whispered cry. *Oh, how wonderful,* she thought, catching her breath as her tears stained the pink, paper heart.

They carried the groceries to the kitchen and exchanged happy squeals as each treasured food item was revealed from the bags.

Stephanie realized most of her neighbors were not members of the Church. *What wonderful people,* she thought. *Will they ever know how much this means to us?* "Oh, how wonderful. But how did they know?" she exclaimed.

The phone rang. "Hello," said Stephanie nearly out of breath from the excitement. The caller was a friend from another ward in their stake.

"Maggie mentioned to me you might be interested in a new job. I'm leaving my work as office manager and wondered if you'd like to come in for an interview with my boss. I can arrange it. I think you'd get the job."

Stephanie was stunned. "Yes, yes. I would like that," she stumbled her words in reply.

"What time do you go to work?"

"I have to be there by 9:00 A.M."

"Can you come in tomorrow before you go to work, say at 8:15? I'll call my boss right now and see if he'll come in early to talk with you."

"Well, yes, definitely, of course I can."

"Okay, unless I call you back otherwise, I'll see you in the morning."

Stephanie got the directions and then hung up the receiver. Her head felt like it was full of effervescent bubbles swirling in sweet pudding.

That evening, family prayer was particularly joyous. There didn't seem to be words sufficient to express enough gratitude, and bedtime hugs were extra strong and energetic.

Monday morning Stephanie attended the job interview and was offered the position at double her present pay.

Her workday was a happy daze. At evening, there were healthy choices for dinner, and the family home evening activity of playing hide-n-seek in the house was filled with the healing medicine of laughter.

As Stephanie readied for bed, she purposely opened her scriptures to read one specific verse—Ether 12:6.

> And now, I, Moroni, would speak somewhat concerning these things; I would show unto the world that faith is things which are hoped for and not seen; wherefore, dispute not because ye see not, for ye receive no witness until after the trial of your faith.

Chapter 7

Writing the rent check on pay day was a celebration. Over the next month the single woman's challenge was not so much how to stretch the money or her time as it was to stretch her thinking. As with any new job, there was much to learn, to sort in priority. She knew the Lord wanted her to succeed. That knowledge was her anchor.

Stephanie concentrated on setting realistic limits and goals. She learned that if she set those boundaries, she was more productive because she wasn't always distracted with making decisions of what to do when. She set Saturday and Sunday as family time and rarely strayed from that routine.

Although the team-work effort of fixing meals and cleaning house didn't always work with the children, it did set up a healthy structure for them. The routine created stability as it became familiar.

She tried to concentrate on work when she was at work. Although she couldn't divorce herself completely from the concerns and worries of home, she tried to break up those thoughts into little blocks of time so she could focus on what needed to be done at work.

To succeed, Stephanie learned the confident body language of a business woman. When at home, that body language dissipated to allow her natural, compassionate, mothering instincts to emerge.

She made strengthening and nurturing her family her first priority. As a family, Stephanie and the children continued their daily family prayers and weekly family home evenings. They read scriptures together and attended their church meetings. When Stephanie drove Eric to special priesthood meetings or Cheri and Alison to extra young women activities, she would say, "Remember, the world belongs to those who show up!"

Stephanie tried to simplify wherever possible. She became better at grouping errands so they took less time. She planned menus that nourished, encouraged order and a clean house, and insisted that the children's school work or other obligations be priorities.

Walking was still a joy to her. She saw the world differently when she took care of herself. She didn't know when it happened, but she realized that at some point she had become more relaxed. The single woman felt happier. She knew she could handle far more than she thought she could only a few weeks earlier.

The amber leaves had long since fallen. Stephanie's envelope budget was a success. With effort, the new job allowed enough for bills to be paid and a small, carefully planned cushion of savings.

Stephanie decided to replace her walking with running now that there was enough money to buy running shoes to protect her feet. She looked forward to each morning's run—how it increased her energy and how alive she felt. She became aware of the movement of her body and how great it felt to use her muscles.

She committed to herself to say her morning prayer before leaving the house to run. She printed a small card with the word "prayer" on it and placed the card on top of her running shoes. Each morning as she put on her shoes, the card acted as a cue reminding her to say her prayer. Running and prayer became synchronized habits.

Stephanie specifically prayed for what she needed help with each day and used her running time to find solutions. As she ran, thoughts—little words or sentences—came to her mind and she filled with resolve knowing how to work through her problems and challenges.

One morning she ran against a strong, horizontal wind blowing from the south. *Wow,* she thought as she pushed her body hard against the wind's resistance trying to maintain forward momentum. *It's almost as though I could lay on the wind. But it wouldn't carry me forward. It would sweep me back.*

She slowed to catch her breath. The wind didn't feel so intense. *Like life's challenges, I've got to lean into the wind as though I'm climbing a hill. I can't let it knock me back. I may slow down but I mustn't stop moving forward.*

Stephanie rounded a street corner, the wind now at her back. *This is how it feels when the children and I work as a team—we move forward with ease.*

"We are all enlisted till the conflict is o'er," hummed Stephanie in her mind. *"Happy are we! Happy are we!"* She concentrated to match her pace

with the beat of the verse. *"Soldiers in the army, there's a bright crown in store; We shall win and wear it by and by. . . . We shall win and wear it by and by . . ."* ("We Are All Enlisted," *Hymns,* no. 250.)

She laughed out loud as she ran past two pennies on the pavement. How good it felt—to laugh. Only a few weeks ago she had stooped to pick up a penny and a nickel longing for support and for burdens to be lifted. The difference between what she thought *ought* to be happening in her life and what *was* happening had been painful. Her new confidence allowed her to let go of what was missing and enjoy reality. Although her load was still heavy and she longed to be an at-home mom, she chose to see her circumstances differently.

"Thank you," she said to her unseen friend as she neared her home. "Thank you, Heavenly Father, for teaching me, for showing me, for helping me grow."

The following Sunday Stephanie decided to read over her conference notes and the goals she had set. She had reviewed them often and incorporated most of them as a regular part of her life.

> *My children and I have strong testimonies of the gospel of Jesus Christ because:*
> *1. I pray for God's influence each morning and thank him each night.*

The favorite parts of my day, Stephanie thought.

> *2. I attend my church meetings regularly.*
> *3. I prepare and present a family home*

> *evening lesson for my family each Sunday,
> or I give my children the opportunity to
> present a lesson.*
> 4. *I read at least one verse from the scriptures
> each evening before I go to bed.*
> 5. *I attend the temple once a month.*

I'll have to work on that one, reflected Stephanie.

> 6. *I pay my tithing.*

Yes!

> *My children know I love them because:*
> 1. *I tell them I love them and touch them with
> a hug or shoulder squeeze at least once a
> day.*
> 2. *I listen and look at them when they speak to
> me.*
> 3. *I catch them doing things right and tell
> them so at least once a day.*
> 4. *We have family prayer together every night;
> everyday in my personal prayers, I ask
> Heavenly Father to bless each of my chil-
> dren.*
> 5. *I advise them, but let them make their own
> decisions and I honor those decisions.*

*That one's hard but I've got to let them have their
agency and love them regardless of their choices.*

> 6. *I meet with each of my children one-on-one
> at least once a month to let them talk about
> how they feel.*

I'd better talk with the children about this.
Resolved, Stephanie thought, *We could start doing it this week.*

> *I keep myself in good physical condition by walking at least six days a week.*

Stephanie rewrote her goal:

> *I keep myself in good physical condition by:*
> *1. Running six days a week.*
> *2. Eating a balanced diet each day.*
> *3. Getting at least seven hours of sleep each night.*

Oh my, that last one will be a challenge!

Later, during the family home evening, Stephanie suggested each of the children individually go with her so they could visit one-on-one during the next month. They could get an ice cream cone or something inexpensive of their choice. "We'll just talk about your goals—what I can do to help—or talk about whatever you want to," she said.

The children liked the idea and they set tentative dates on the calendar, starting with Cheri.

Stephanie tried to be consistent and follow through with the things she told the children she would do. During their one-on-one time together, Stephanie asked the children what they would like to talk about. She always reminded them to say their personal prayers and that each of them was valuable and worthwhile. Even if she was upset with one of them because of their behavior, she would end with a big hug, look them straight in the eye, and say "I love you" so they would know she was really on their side. She wanted them to know what was expected of them, and that no matter what happened, they were loved.

One morning, when the single woman was at work, she received an urgent phone call from Cheri. "You've got to come home right now, Mom. We've been robbed! We've been robbed," she repeated with obvious trembling.

"Have you called the police?"

"No."

"All right. You call the police, and I'll be right there." Stephanie hurriedly explained the need for her rapid exit and rushed home.

When she arrived, she found Cheri in a daze, Eric and Alison not yet home from school.

"What happened, Cheri?"

"I don't know. I came home at lunch time, as usual. The back door, where I always enter, was locked. Everything looked fine. I ate my lunch. Then I got my bracelet out of my bedroom, locked the back door, and left through the front door.

"The front door was unlocked. Eric was the last one out this morning. I figured he must have forgotten to lock it. So I locked it behind me.

"After school, I entered by way of the back door again, which I distinctly remember locking at lunch time. But it wasn't latched. It opened freely. Then I knew something was wrong. I was really mad.

"The kitchen cupboards were open. They even took all the groceries you bought last night, Mom!

"I went through the house hoping to catch the robbers."

"You did what? Why didn't you call the police right then?" squealed Stephanie.

"I was just so mad," Cheri shouted. "Our VCR is gone. They took all my new clothes—the ones that still had the tags on from yesterday's shopping. My camera's gone, all my jewelry," she cried, shaking with anger.

Stephanie put her arms around her daughter. "It's okay. Calm down. We'll make it through this too," she said softly.

Just then Eric and Alison arrived home from school. "What are you doing home, Mom? What? What's going on?" Eric asked excitedly, seeing Cheri cry in her mother's arms.

"You left the front door open. Someone got in and robbed us," accused Cheri.

"But I didn't," frowned Eric. "I locked the door when I left this morning. I didn't forget, Mom!" protested Eric.

"Okay. Let's carefully go through the house. Just look with your eyes. Don't disturb anything until the police get here. Maybe there'll be some finger prints," Stephanie warned.

Eric discovered the dirty clothes dumped out in his bedroom, the bag missing. Alison found her money, camera, and jewelry also gone. Stephanie's jewelry box drawers were empty, everything missing including her wedding ring.

By the time the police officer arrived, they had determined about $2000 of belongings had been taken. With no renter's insurance, there could be no immediate replacements. The mystery remained, however, of how the robbers had entered.

The officer dusted for prints, but only found smudges. "Your son must have accidentally left the door unlocked," the police officer suggested. "I see no forced entry."

"But I didn't," Eric passionately insisted.

"How then?" questioned the officer.

"I saw a show on television last week," Alison suddenly interrupted, "where the robbers got in through a little, doggie door."

Stephanie's eyes opened wide. "We have one," she exclaimed. "Wait. We have one!" She rushed into her bedroom. A large, sliding glass door offering an exit to the back porch filled half the back wall space. In front of the glass door was a table. Behind the table, at the extreme corner of the glass door, was a tiny, pet door.

"But I just checked that the other day," Stephanie said.

On hands and knees she climbed under the table. The boxes she had stacked there had been moved, a ruler knocked to the floor, and the miniature door slightly ajar.

"But how? How could anyone fit through that door?" asked Stephanie.

After investigating, the officer said, "It's not uncommon. Robbers can jimmy this type of latch easily. They can send a child or small teen through the opening to unlock the front door of the house from the inside and let the others in.

"I'd have that little door replaced if I were you," he added calmly.

"Looks like they emptied your laundry bag and used it to carry the things; must have dumped the jewelry boxes upside down and gone through your closets and drawers pretty well."

"But when?" questioned Stephanie. "Do you think they were in the house when Cheri came home for lunch?"

"Yes. I'd say you're pretty fortunate, young lady," the officer stated flatly to Cheri. "They must have already let the older or larger ones in the front door before you got home the first time. Maybe they were hiding in your mom's bedroom. If they were quiet, you wouldn't have seen or heard them there. After you ate your lunch and left, they robbed you, and left by way of the back door."

Stephanie looked at Cheri, realizing the danger she had been in.

"But my clothes," wailed Cheri.

"The clothes are nothing," said Stephanie. "We can eventually replace clothes. We could never replace you. At least you weren't hurt.

"People are more important than things," said Stephanie, holding Cheri snugly.

Looking over Cheri's shoulder, Stephanie saw her running shoes still in their place by the back door.

Oh, thank you, she thought. *Thank you. At least they didn't take my running shoes! At least they didn't take that away from me. With my running shoes and my Heavenly Father, I can work through anything,* Stephanie smiled.

"You weren't hurt—that's all that matters," she said softly but clearly to Cheri. "Piece by piece we will accumulate the things again."

Several days passed to dull the shock. Each member of the family repeated telling about the incident many times to friends and neighbors. Stephanie tried to help the children discover the value of a good attitude—a grateful attitude—by looking past the apparent bad to the good in the situation. She stressed what wasn't taken.

"At least they left the TV! Look, Ali, your favorite cereal is still here!"

Cheri remained in mourning over her departed clothes, but in the days that followed, she came to appreciate the miracle of her safety.

The following Sunday was fast and testimony day. As usual, Stephanie and her little family attended sacrament meeting. The single woman smiled as she stood and nervously walked to the microphone to share her testimony.

"Satan would lead us to believe we do not have time to be friendly, to do for others, and to share of ourselves," Stephanie cleared her throat. "But the Lord would tell us to reach out with love and with an example of integrity.

"Most often it is the little things we do for others that fill in the cracks. But Cathy, Pearl, and Joyce, and perhaps more of you than I'm aware of, took action in a big way to fill a large crack.

"Thank you for the food you and other neighbors left on our doorstep a couple months ago. Your action directly answered my prayer and provided a much needed bridge to my belated pay day.

"This past week, several of you filled another crack. My children and I were robbed. You provided a different kind of bridge by letting us talk—helping us work through the emotions of our loss.

"Yesterday a Primary sister mentioned to me that Alison needed to work on her Articles of Faith. That is a crack. This sister's reminder will help me fill that crack if I make the effort to work with Alison and prioritize the Articles of Faith into our family home evening lessons.

"Thank you for doing what you do to build and buoy us up. But the bottom line is, it is my responsibility to develop me, to make things right for me and my family. I am accountable for what I believe and how I act. In the long run, I personally have to make the effort to feed my family, to have a grateful attitude, so your work and friendship can seep in and seal the cracks, and so the cracks don't become overwhelming voids."

The gleam in Stephanie's eye reflected her hard-earned, personal sense of self reliance. "We help each other along. At times we may even carry each other, but we cannot continually expect others to sustain us. Each of us must make our own destiny by the choices we personally make. Those big canyons we each have to cross depend on our putting forth the effort ourselves and leaning on the Lord.

"I need to put forth the effort to know the scriptures, attend my meetings, and pray so I will have a firm base to work from to solve my problems. It is up to me to gain a testimony, up to me to take proper care of my body, and up to me to welcome your friendship. Then the impossible, unbelievable things that happen to me will not bury me.

"I have a testimony the Lord really knows the details of my life. I have faith in the Lord and literally expect His help. I will do everything I can alone, then I will lean on Him and He will help me to know who to reach out to or He will bring me aid.

"It's like trying to travel by foot through a dark tunnel, but you can't see a light at the other end." Stephanie hesitated as tears welled in her eyes. She reached for a tissue from the box placed on the podium. "If you put forth the effort to move your feet while you blindly, in faith, hold on to the sides of the tunnel to guide you, you'll finally reach a point where the light at the end of the tunnel is obvious.

"You know how people talk about seeing their lives from the viewpoint of a *half full* glass of water or a *half empty* glass of water? Well, some people, through no fault of their own, have a *completely empty* glass. It's bone dry!

"If we find ourselves in that kind of situation, it's up to us to look for a faucet—and maybe even a hand to help us turn the handle of the faucet to fill our glass again. *But we have to do the reaching!*

"Many times this past year I thought I could not sustain any more. As I would pray, I would ask, 'I have done all I can do. You know I am at my limit. Please send me help.' I remember one incident in particular when I knew I had reached my limit. Then our wonderful Relief Society president called. She said, 'You've been on my mind . . .'

"I reached for the faucet. Through the Lord's intervention, Maggie helped me turn the handle of the faucet to fill my glass.

"The other day as I started out for my morning run, the clouds covered the distant mountains. On my way back, the cloud cover had shifted and I could see the very top of the mountain peaking through the heavy, white clouds. Everything below was covered as if with a layer of thick quilt batting.

"I couldn't help but think how the scene was so much like life—how we mustn't let our problems cloud our judgment; how we mustn't loose sight of our goals. We've got to keep our focus on reaching the top of each of our own magnificent mountains.

"I'm thankful for what I've learned, for experience, for growth. I know myself better, and I know God better. I know God gives inspiration and revelation today. I know He knows me and my family, and is aware of our needs. I know the Lord has clearly answered my prayers without fail," Stephanie stated firmly.

"I know if I continue to do everything I can; if I put in my share of the effort, my Heavenly Father will show me the path I personally should follow to fulfill the mission I am accountable for."

Stephanie returned to her seat. From her left side she heard Cheri softly say, "Good job!"

On her right, Eric whispered, "Way to go, Mom."

Stephanie caught the feeling of happiness offered by Alison's beaming smile.

At evening, as she readied for bed, she reflected on what she had said when bearing her testimony, ". . . my Heavenly Father will show me the path I personally should follow to fulfill the mission I am accountable for."

Stephanie removed her patriarchal blessing from the pocket of her scriptures. Reading it thoughtfully, she mulled over each phrase referring to a righteous companion and her activities in conjunction with that worthy person. *How can I fulfill my mission? I don't have a worthy companion. How can I trust again? Is it possible to have a relationship absent of deceit, manipulation, or hitting? How can I find love—a feeling of truly being loved?*

Stephanie read her patriarchal blessing a second time. *He is promised there for me,* she thought. *But how do I find him?*

She knelt in the familiar attitude of prayer. "Heavenly Father, thank you for all your help. Thank you for protection. Thank you for my children.

"I've been reading my patriarchal blessing. Will you please reveal to me what your plan is for me? I don't see how I can fulfill what is written here. If this is my mission, what am I supposed to do to make it happen? How can it happen?"

At the conclusion of her prayer, she reached for her scriptures. Once again she let the scriptures randomly fall open to select a verse. She read the highlighted passage:

> And it came to pass that I, Nephi, said unto my father: I will go and do the things which the Lord hath commanded, for I know that the Lord giveth no commandments unto the children of men, save he shall prepare a way for them that they may accomplish the thing which he commandeth them. (I Nephi 3:7.)

She smiled, shaking her head. *How?* she questioned. *How? I don't even know anyone,* she reasoned as she fell asleep.

The next morning, Stephanie arose a little earlier than usual to fit in her morning run. Because of a deadline she would have to leave for work half an hour sooner than she was accustomed.

She took the cue from the prayer card placed atop her running shoes and knelt beside the couch to ask for protection. "It's dark out," she said. "Please bless me with safety as I run—that no harm of any kind will befall me. And please help me to know what I can do so my patriarchal blessing can be fulfilled."

The sun had not even risen enough to cast a silhouette of the distant mountains to the east. The bright, snow-white moon peered over the tips of the jagged mountain peaks in the west.

Stephanie was so used to her running route, she didn't mind the dark. "I don't see how it can happen," she said in a breathy whisper. "I don't date. . . . I don't even know anyone to date. . . . How?"

Whoosh.

What? What happened?

Stunned for a moment, Stephanie felt as though she were in a vacuum—everything around her in slow motion. She heard nothing, only felt the overwhelming realization that she had been moved. So completely occupied by her thoughts, she hadn't been paying attention. Because of the early hour, no cars in sight, she had been running on the road in the traffic lane when she felt herself suddenly moved over and a car speeding by. Had she not been moved, certainly the car would have hit her.

Stephanie was overcome with the magnitude of what had happened. *He moved me . . . me . . . He actually moved me over.*

Running slowly, she thought of nothing else for the next several blocks. Then the thought came to her: *If He has the power to move me, to save my life, He has the power to choreograph the happenings of my days*

*and my weeks for my patriarchal blessing to be ful-
filled. He knows me. He even knows my thoughts. . . .
He picked me up and moved me on the road. . . . If I
keep the commandments and trust Him, He can make it
all happen.*

Light emerged from behind the mountains as
though someone turned up a dimmer switch. The rum-
pled, gray clouds were over-painted with pink. As the
sky brightened, the pink carried a golden cast sharply
contrasting the darkness of the mountains below. The
light quickly filtered across rich aqua-blue patches of
sky and hope crept into Stephanie's heart.

"We are all enlisted till the conflict is o'er,"
hummed Stephanie. *"Happy are we! Happy are we!
Soldiers in the army, there's a bright crown in store; We
shall win and wear it by and by.*

*"Dangers may gather—why should we fear? Jesus,
our Leader, ever is near. He will protect us, comfort,
and cheer. We're joyfully, joyfully marching to our
home. We are all enlisted till the conflict is o'er; Happy
are we! Happy are we! Soldiers in the army, there's a
bright crown in store; We shall win and wear it by and
by."* ("We Are All Enlisted," *Hymns,* no. 250.)

Chapter 8

The day passed quickly for the single woman. At evening, she reviewed her goals:

> *My children and I have strong testimonies of the gospel of Jesus Christ because:*
> 1. *I pray for God's influence each morning and thank him each night.*
> 2. *I attend my church meetings regularly.* ·
> 3. *I prepare and present a family home evening lesson for my family each Sunday, or I give my children the opportunity to present a lesson.*
> 4. *I read at least one verse from the scriptures each evening before I go to bed.*
> 5. *I attend the temple once a month.*

Let me see, she thought as she turned to her calendar, *what day can I go to the temple? Eric's ball game is Wednesday . . . Thursday, I'll go Thursday night.*

> 6. *I pay my tithing.*

Stephanie hesitated for a moment, then wrote:

> 7. *I do my part to see my patriarchal blessing fulfilled.*

Reconsidering, she added:

*7. **I pray each day that my mission be made clear to me;** I do my part **each day** to see that my patriarchal blessing is fulfilled.*

Writing slowly, she amended her goal sheet once again:

8. I am married to a worthy companion who holds and honors the priesthood.

Stephanie stared at the sentence and read it over in her mind, then reviewed the remaining goals.

My children know I love them because:
1. I tell them I love them and touch them with a hug or shoulder squeeze at least once a day.
2. I listen and look at them when they speak to me.
3. I catch them doing things right and tell them so at least once a day.
4. We have family prayer together every night; everyday in my personal prayers, I ask Heavenly Father to bless each of my children.
5. I advise them, but let them make their own decisions and I honor those decisions.
6. I meet with each of my children one-on-one at least once a month to let them talk about how they feel.

I keep myself in good physical condition by:
1. Running six days a week.

2. *Eating a balanced diet each day.*
3. *Getting at least seven hours of sleep each night.*

Stephanie reread her new goals:

7. *I pray each day that my mission be made clear to me; I do my part each day to see that my patriarchal blessing is fulfilled.*
8. *I am married to a worthy companion who holds and honors the priesthood.*

When? How? I can't put a date on it. She pulled out her patriarchal blessing from the scripture pocket.

". . . In the due time of the Lord, you will have a companion, one that will be worthy to go to the House of the Lord, and there you will receive your privileges and blessings and be sealed for time and for all eternity."

In the temple . . . I will marry him in the temple.

Stephanie reached for the telephone. "Hello, Oma? I hope I'm not calling too late."

"No. It's fine," responded the soft, familiar voice.

"I was wondering if I could come over tomorrow. Would your husband give me a blessing?"

"Of course," Oma responded immediately. "When would you like to come?"

"Tomorrow's Saturday. I don't have to work. What time is good for you?"

Stephanie heard Oma relay the question to her husband, then answer, "How about seven tomorrow evening?"

"Thank you, Oma. I'll see you then."

That night the single woman had a restless sleep. She found herself excited about the next day—about seeing Oma and her husband and about the priesthood blessing she would receive.

When the single woman arrived at Oma's home, the sun was setting and the porch light was on. Oma greeted her with a warm smile, "My it's good to see you. How are the children?"

"Fine. They're fine," Stephanie replied.

"How are you doing?" Oma asked eagerly.

"I need help, Oma. I don't know what I'm supposed to do."

"Hello," Stephanie said as Oma's husband joined them in the living room.

"I overheard your concern from the kitchen. Tell me what's troubling you," said Oma's husband.

"My patriarchal blessing talks about me having a worthy companion. Will you give me a blessing to help me know what I'm supposed to do?"

Stephanie related the experience she had earlier in the week of being moved while running. "I know God can choreograph things to make it happen if I am worthy. But maybe I'm not good enough. And what's my part? What am I supposed to do?" the single woman asked.

"Much of my previous marriage I felt like I was balancing on one foot while holding in my hands a very heavy, yet thin and fragile, crystal bowl. Many times my body felt so tired of continually holding that pose, I wanted to drop the bowl and relax my legs. I felt like my husband, because of his decisions and actions, yanked the bowl out of my grasp and threw it to the ground, shattering it in a thousand pieces—like my life was totally out of my control . . . a complete loss of trust.

"I felt blinded. I wanted to put on some glasses that would make it possible for me to clearly see why he had made those decisions. I wanted to read his mind as clearly as I could read a page.

"Oma, you once told me you can't make others' choices for them; that he had the right to choose his reward by his actions. But what if it happens again? I can't make it if it happens a second time," cried Stephanie.

Oma's husband rested his hand on her shoulder and asked for her full name, then began the blessing. As he spoke, a calm, sweet spirit replaced Stephanie's feeling of mild panic.

"Stephanie, your Heavenly Father loves you very much. Put your anxiety at rest. Be peaceful, very peaceful. He is pleased with you and your efforts. You are doing all the right things. You are getting your life in balance by taking good care of yourself and your family. Continue in patience. And go with a light heart.

"Cease to worry. There is a worthy companion being prepared for you—a companion who truly has a testimony and commitment to the gospel—a man with root integrity, who places his relationship with the Lord first—someone who will offer honest, true companionship, a full commitment, and open communication.

"He will financially support you and your family. He is someone you can safely respect and love—someone your children can respect and love.

"You must exercise your faith and be patient. He is not ready to receive you. He will love you and he will love your children as his own.

"I bless you to think clearly, to know the activities you should pursue to find your companion. Listen with the Spirit instead of with your head. As it is written in Proverbs, 'Trust in the Lord with all thine heart; and lean not unto thine own understanding. In all thy ways acknowledge him, and he shall direct they path.' (Proverbs 3:5.)

"Satan wants you to remember the failure—to fear the future, the unknown. It is natural for you to have some fear. But don't let it control you. Your Heavenly Father wants you to succeed; the only way to overcome fear is through complete trust in Him. Keep your eyes on the prize and be open to seeing the beauty around you.

"I bless you to know what you are supposed to do. You will know without doubt who the right one is. You will feel a stupor of thought when situations and individuals aren't right for you.

"I promise that in the Lord's time, the blessings you seek (the righteous desires of your heart), through patience and peace, will be rewarded to you."

The blessing concluded, Stephanie said, "Thank

you," as she shook the gentle man's hand. "What I need is a Liahona!"

"But you have one," the man insisted with a smile.

"Do you know what it is?" asked Oma.

"Yes," Stephanie answered, "the Holy Ghost."

"It's simple," said Oma's husband. "If you are faithful, the Holy Ghost will direct your path just as surely as that compass pointed the way for the Nephites."

"And it will work for you," Oma said, "if you choose to listen and embrace the promptings."

The single woman nodded her agreement and said, "I know how it works.

"Thank you for the beautiful blessing," Stephanie said to Oma's husband.

"I'm excited for you," exclaimed Oma with a hug. "Those are powerful promises."

Stephanie waved good-bye to her friends as she drove away from the hilltop home. The lights of the city below shown like bright, colored gems in a jewel chest. She stopped the car by the roadside to reflect on the words of the blessing.

"I wonder," she said out loud. "What does he look like? When? How?"

Sitting in silence, she felt the distinct impression that she would some day live at the foot of the distant mountains across the valley.

In the weeks that followed, Stephanie prayed earnestly for direction. She observed the limited number of single men attending her ward, and asked friends and family if they knew anyone eligible.

She knew what she was looking for—an unquestionably active member of the Church, someone who believed in family and motherhood, someone without guile.

Stephanie attended singles' firesides and dinners. At one point, Cheri even attended a sacrament meeting at a singles' ward with her so she wouldn't have to attend alone. As Stephanie looked over the audience, she couldn't help but think how sad it was that so many families had been disrupted by divorce or death—that so many people must feel as alone as she did, even in a crowd.

She never dated anyone more than twice. By that time, their conversations revealed a difference in values and commitment, an evident difference in perspective and goals. But she felt so sure that this was the time to meet *him,* she began fasting every Sunday, praying for the Lord to direct her to her promised companion and he to her.

Stephanie worked with her schedule to make sure she was able to attend the temple. She went every month, once a month, alone. During one of her monthly visits, she suddenly felt an unmistakable awareness, almost like words being spoken, yet it wasn't. It was matter of fact and disconnected to the temple presentation. It was the distinct feeling that soon she would not be alone attending the temple—consistently someone would be with her—a worthy companion.

She looked on both sides of her to see if the ladies sitting next to her heard her chuckle. *I'm not even regularly dating anyone,* she laughed at herself. *How could it be that I would soon come here with a companion? That's going to take time.*

Stephanie thought of how sure she felt while bearing her testimony only a few short months ago. *It seems as though I ride a roller coaster with my faith,* she reflected, *strong and weak, strong and weak. Why do I doubt? After all I've experienced, why, how can I question it?*

The sweet confidence and peace she felt sharpened her belief that a companion was being prepared for her, as Oma's husband had promised in the blessing. She didn't know how it would happen, but felt if she exercised her faith, the Lord would move her in a position for the promises to be kept. And soon, very soon, she wouldn't be coming to the temple alone.

A week later, Stephanie answered the ring of her home telephone. "Hello."

"Stephanie?"

"Yes."

"My name is Kris. I'm calling from the Area Dating Service. Your name was given to me from a friend. I think we can help you. Would you like to come in for a free consultation?"

"It doesn't cost anything?" Stephanie asked.

"That's right. The consultation is free."

What can it hurt? Stephanie thought. *Maybe I'll learn something about myself that will help me in dating.* "Okay," Stephanie agreed.

"Thursday?"

"Yes. That will be fine."

"Five-thirty?"

"Yes. I'll be there."

Thursday arrived quickly. Stephanie met with the representative who explained their services. The representative spoke as though she really understood the trials of trying to find that illusive life-puzzle piece—a loyal mate. They visited about two hours before Kris told Stephanie the price of their dating service.

Stephanie laughed out loud, "I don't have that kind of money. You don't get the picture do you? I'm a single mom providing for a family alone. I don't have that kind of money," she repeated.

Kris said, "I'll tell you what. I really feel strongly you should be in this program. I'm pretty sure if I talk to my manager, he'll agree to give you a special deal. Wait here and I'll be right back."

Kris left Stephanie alone in the small, conference room but returned before Stephanie could reason her way clear to leave.

"He said he could let you join for this amount." Kris showed Stephanie a price sheet with the original price considerably marked down.

Stephanie shook her head. "You still don't get it do you? See," Stephanie remarked as she pulled open her checkbook to reveal the balance in her account. "See? This is all I have. And I still have groceries to buy and the children's' shoes to pay for. This is all I've got."

"Stay here. I'll talk to my manager again," said Kris. "But I don't think he'll agree to that," she whispered as though to herself as she left the room.

Stephanie was amazed at herself that she sat there, that Kris would even consider her a candidate to pay money for anything beyond the immediate needs of her family. She thought she and Kris had gotten to know each other better than that during their lengthy visit.

When Kris returned, she was carrying a camera. "I can't believe he said 'yes.' But he said if you give what you have in your account and agree to pay $20 every month for a year, he'll let you join. Here's the form to sign."

Stephanie was caught off guard. Almost in a stupor, she signed the paper and wrote out the check.

Kris said, "Stand there against the wall so I can take your picture. It will be a temporary picture in your portfolio until you come for the photography session. Call tomorrow for an appointment. Fill out this questionnaire and bring it back as soon as possible so we can put your information in the portfolio book.

"This is how it works," Kris continued as she gave Stephanie a tour of the facility. "Your portfolio pages are placed in these books alphabetically by first name. Your last name, address, and phone number aren't given out until you agree to a date. There are over 500 men's portfolios shown in this library. You can look through them any time you want.

"Each person also has a video, so you can observe body language and know what the individual sounds like. Here's the list of questions you'll be asked when you're video taped.

"When you find someone you're interested in by studying their portfolio pages and watching their video, turn in a request at the front desk. The dating service will notify the man you've selected and he'll come in and look at your portfolio and video. He let's us know if he wants to meet you. If he does, we give you both each other's last name and phone number, and you meet over the phone to arrange your date.

"Of course it works in reverse. If a man comes in and sees your video and wants to meet you, you'll be contacted and have the opportunity to say 'yes' or 'no.'"

Stephanie left with her stack of papers to read and questions to answer.

At home, she apologized repeatedly to the children. "I can't believe I'm doing this. I've heard horror stories about dating services. I'm sorry. I'm always so careful with the money. How can I do this?"

"It's okay, Mom. We'll all help. We can make it," said Cheri. "What kind of questions are there?"

"It asks for my short-term goals and a separate list of my long-term goals. It asks what three attributes I'm looking for in the ideal companion, whether my goal of dating is marriage, and whether I like to travel. Here's a question, 'What are the most important things to you?' And this one, 'What would people be surprised to know about you?'

"I'm not even sure how to answer some of these," Stephanie shook her head.

Cheri laughed, "Come on. I'll help you. Let's fill out the forms so you can take them in tomorrow!"

With Cheri quizzing her mother, they completed the lengthy questionnaire and developed a list of criteria to follow when looking through portfolios.

The next morning Stephanie called for a late-afternoon photography appointment. Cheri agreed to go with her.

After the pictures were taken and Stephanie's interview in front of the video camera was completed, Cheri and her mother entered the portfolio library.

"Let's only look at the ones in this age category," Stephanie said pointing to the criteria list she had placed on the table between them. "How about you take this stack and I'll go through these?"

Mother and daughter giggled as they opened the portfolios stacked in front of them. Each time they found a profile describing a man the desired age, they stopped and together determined from his written answers if he was a member of the Church. If they thought *yes*, they looked for an indication he liked children. Then they determined whether his income was sufficient to support a family.

If he passed all the above, they compared his profile ratings with Stephanie's. The dating service had provided a wallet-sized card with a list of findings based on how the individual had answered the questionnaire. The findings covered 15 areas including work values, morality, religious convictions, and possessiveness.

"Oh, look at this one," Cheri giggled. "This one's cute, Mom."

"No," Stephanie laughed, "follow the criteria. The way he looks comes last!"

Only a few men passed this initial screening. Stephanie and Cheri went into the video room to see what they could learn by watching the men answer the script questions in front of a camera. One man looked too much like Stephanie's previous husband. Another never smiled and kept repeating himself. When asked, "What do you like to do in your spare time?" he answered in a monotone voice, "I like to garden."

"What would people be surprised to know about you?"

"I like to garden."

"Describe yourself in one or two words."

"I like to garden."

"Do you consider yourself romantic?"

"No."

"That's enough of that," laughed Stephanie as she rewound and ejected the tape.

"Okay, how about this one?" Cheri said as she put in the next video.

Stephanie looked at the screen. "This . . . this man . . .," she stammered, "he's the one standing on the ladder."

"What are you talking about, Mom?"

"Remember?" Stephanie said in a hushed, excited voice. "Remember when I went to that conference? I told you about him. He stood on a ladder wearing a gold cape!"

Stephanie leaned over to look at his portfolio page in the notebook spread across Cheri's lap. She read the question: "What is your favorite quote?"

His written reply was something he had said at the conference. "My favorite quote is by Brent A. Barlow: 'What we are is more important than what we have been. And what we can become is more important than what we are.'"

Chapter 9

His name was David. When they visited on the telephone to arrange a date, he explained that Kris, at the dating service, told him about Stephanie. He joined the day before she did; that was how his request to meet her got processed before her request to meet him.

The first date, David stood on the doorstep dressed in a dark suit, handing Stephanie a dozen tissue-wrapped, red roses.

Maybe I should have dressed up more, the single woman thought as she invited him in, thanked him for the roses, and laid them down on the lamp table. Having never been to the restaurant they were going to, she hadn't known what to wear. A white blouse and blue dress pants were the final choice. Cheri had picked out the gold earrings.

"I attended the singles' conference last fall," she said. "You did a great job."

"Front row, right?" David quizzed with a smile. "You were wearing this same white blouse, weren't you? But with a dark pinstripe skirt."

"Well, maybe . . . yes, . . . I guess I was," she stammered returning his smile.

He was taller than she remembered. She felt peace and energy around him just as she had at the conference.

"These are my daughters, Cheri and Alison, and my son, Eric."

"Happy to meet you."

"Shall we go?" Stephanie awkwardly suggested.

"Aren't you going to put them in water?" he asked pointing to the roses.

"Oh, yes," Stephanie answered. She had promised herself to be a data collector for the evening and was focusing so heavily on the questions she wanted to ask, she completely forgot about the roses.

Embarrassed, Stephanie handed the flowers to Cheri. "Could you put these in water for me, please?"

"Sure Mom," giggled Cheri.

It was a small restaurant with an elegant, unrushed environment. David said that was why he had selected it. He wanted them both to feel comfortable and unhurried so they could visit.

Several hours of examination passed, the food hardly noticed. He seemed to have as many questions for her as she did for him! They covered more than the memorized list Stephanie carried in her head.

"Would you like to see where I work?" David asked.

"I'd like that," said Stephanie.

They continued the exchange of information as he drove her by his office, then to his home. After a brief introduction of David's children, he escorted Stephanie to the patio.

Casually they talked for some time before Stephanie said, "It's been a lovely evening. I think I'd better go now."

She had gathered more information than she bargained for. *My brain's on overload,* she thought. *I need to leave so I can decipher what I've learned.*

David drove her home and accompanied her to the front door. Awkwardly, cautiously, he offered a hand shake to say good-bye.

Even with the late hour, when Stephanie entered the house, her children were waiting anxiously for a report.

"What was he like?" asked Alison.

"What was the restaurant like? What did you eat?" quizzed Eric.

"Did you meet his children?" asked Cheri.

Stephanie patiently described the events of the evening, followed by family prayer and hugs.

As she knelt by her bedside to end the day, Stephanie first thanked her Heavenly Father. "Thank you for a fun evening. Thank you for my children. Thank you for my job." Then again she verbally revealed her fear and pleaded for His help. "Dear Father, I'm scared. Please help me to not be deceived by others nor to deceive myself. Please help me to exercise the power of discernment you have promised me—to know the truth and to recognize and trust real promptings from the Holy Ghost. Please help me to see things as they really are, to receive the right signals, and to not make a mistake. I love you, Father. I know you are there. Thank you."

The following day, Stephanie called David from her office to invite him to join her family at a friend's home for a picnic and a volleyball game. The evening gave Stephanie the opportunity to observe David's interaction with Cheri, Eric, and Alison. Once again she promised to not be distracted by emotion, to be objective and remain fully aware of his actions and reactions.

He was patient. He was considerate. He had a wonderful sense of humor. Though not a great athlete, he was a good sport. Her friends liked him. Her children enjoyed being with him.

When they arrived home, David said goodnight to the children and they went in. Stephanie and David sat on the porch steps several hours in continued questioning. Before he left, however, David gave Stephanie a light, careful kiss.

As the weeks passed, although Stephanie received other invitations from men through the dating service, she determined by reading the portfolios or listening to the answers on the videos that their spiritual values, their goals, didn't fit what she was after. One man indicated he liked a good party with drink and didn't care what religion his date espoused. Another didn't even enjoy children.

But with David, it was comfortable. It was obvious they enjoyed doing the same things. They shared laughter and a commitment to family. Communication seemed easy and natural. Stephanie felt she could be herself—that she could tell him anything without judgment or criticism. And she felt no need to criticize him because she liked him as he was.

David invited Stephanie on a jeep ride and picnic in the mountains. Stephanie knew they'd have a good time. She loved to be with him.

Is it okay? she prayed in her mind as she sat on the carpeted stairs inside the house with a clear view out the window to the driveway, waiting for him to come. *Can I relax the questions? Is it okay to be attracted to him and let myself feel romantic?*

The blue jeep arrived. David stepped around the jeep, his long stride making short the distance to the front door. *It's okay,* she heard in her mind. A warm flood of attraction flowed from her feet to her knees to her heart. *It's okay.*

They drove to the snow line on the mountain. David spread a blanket and Stephanie served the meal she'd prepared. Though the early-summer sun was bright, the day was cool. The view of the valley below was clear and the background, babbling sounds of pure, flowing water from an underground spring set the mood for David's question.

"It feels right, you and I," he said wrapping an extra blanket about her shoulders. "I figure when it feels right, you shouldn't wait. You should move ahead with things."

Stephanie looked at the intent expression in David's eyes, not sure she was prepared for what he was saying. Her mind raced in reflection of all she had heard. Her thoughts were interwoven with words from Oma and her husband, *'Listen with the Spirit instead of with your head. . . . I bless you to know what you are supposed to do. You will know without doubt who the right one is.'*

"Will you marry me?" David asked. "Will you go to the temple with me and be my wife?"

It wasn't a loud, sharp voice telling her what was right. She immediately recalled the scripture she had read just the night before, 'but the Lord was not in the wind: and after the wind an earthquake; but the Lord was not in the earthquake: and after the earthquake a fire; but the Lord was not in the fire: and after the fire a still small voice.' (1 Kings 1911–12.)

Stephanie felt no need for hesitation. She knew she could trust that still small voice. "Yes," she said willingly. "Yes, I will."

His embrace was no surprise, the kiss sweet, full. They gently fell to the blanket-covered ground. His arm acted as a soft, protective pillow beneath her head. Gently, the tears crept down her cheeks and she knew her answer was right.

They laid there watching the scant, white clouds cross the sky. They planned what they would say to their children, where they would be wed—which temple, and where they would live.

The following week David took Stephanie to the temple on a date. She was distracted as she recalled laughing at herself in that very room just over a month before. It seemed so unlikely then, so impossible that someone, a worthy companion, would consistently be with her. And yet, here she was just as the prompting had said. Without a fanfare of blaring trumpets, it happened quietly, unfolding naturally in her life. The still small voice was true.

That evening Stephanie spread out her goal sheets to read.

> *My children and I have strong testimonies of the gospel of Jesus Christ because:*
> 1. *I pray for God's influence each morning and thank him each night.*
> 2. *I attend my church meetings regularly.*
> 3. *I prepare and present a family home evening lesson for my family each Sunday, or I give my children the opportunity to present a lesson.*
> 4. *I read at least one verse from the scriptures each evening before I go to bed.*
> 5. *I attend the temple once a month.*
> 6. *I pay my tithing.*
> 7. *I pray each day that my mission be made clear to me; I do my part each day to see that my patriarchal blessing is fulfilled.*
> 8. *I am married to a worthy companion who holds and honors the priesthood.*

Slowly, enunciating each word, Stephanie read the eighth goal again and dated it.

> 8. ***October 6,*** *I am married to a worthy companion who holds and honors the priesthood.*

In the morning, Stephanie ran as usual. As she left the house, vague apprehension filled her thoughts. She remembered saying to Oma, *'Oma, you once told me you can't make others' choices for them; that he had the right to choose his reward by his actions. But what if it happens again? I can't make it if it happens a second time.'*

Stephanie neared the vacant lot. The waist-high, tall grasses were replaced by a bed of yellow sunflowers spread like a cheerful blanket of hope.

I can't make David's choices either, she thought. Then holding out her arms, stretching as she ran, she exclaimed out loud, "But I own my world. I know my Heavenly Father loves me and sustains me. I'd follow the same path again and I'd make it!"

"I know you love me," she shouted with a broad smile looking at the blank, powder-blue sky.

'Cease to worry,' she thought. *The priesthood blessing promised. 'There is a worthy companion being prepared for you—a companion who truly has a testimony and commitment to the gospel; a man with root integrity, who places his relationship with the Lord first; someone who will offer honest, true companionship, a full commitment, and open communication.'*

Now as Stephanie walked around her yard to cool down after her run, just thinking of David was calming. *One more month,* she thought. One more month and she would be wed.

Stephanie's stake president marveled how rapidly her sealing clearance came through. In a few short weeks she stepped over the threshold into the temple to covenant with her new companion—a single woman no more.

She felt worthy to be David's companion; she felt the Lord moved them into each other's path; without her manipulation or control, they had come together fitting as naturally as skin draped over a body's unique frame, in perfect harmony.

The soft, gentle voice of the white-haired temple officiator called them to the altar. Although not strikingly beautiful, Stephanie felt elegant wearing the new, white dress she had made. Cheri had helped her by sewing the pearl beads ornamenting the wide collar.

"If either of you have any reservations, if you are not fully committed to this marriage, I want you to feel free to get up and leave now."

Stephanie looked around the room. Oma, her husband, and Stephanie's dear family and friends were startled by the officiator's beginning words. David's gentle stroke on her hand brought her gaze to his kind, peaceful smile. Stephanie instantly reciprocated. They knelt secure, hands clasped over the altar.

"Well then, with that decided, I'll go on!" exclaimed the officiator. The gathered group in the large temple sealing room chuckled freely.

"This cannot be just a contractual agreement between you two," the officiator explained. "You see, this is a covenant you are making with God."

"Contractual agreements are broken so easily. People just walk away when troubles come. But when you make a covenant, you give all you have to work through those troubles. You are bound. Together you discover bridges to cross life's unexpected ravines. And there will be many. As a matter of fact, as your lives unfold, you will travel down roads you haven't even yet identified as a part of your map!

"Elder Orson F. Whitney said, 'No pain that we suffer, no trial that we experience is wasted. It ministers to our education, to the development of such qualities as patience, faith, fortitude and humility. All that we suffer and all that we endure, especially when we endure it patiently, builds up our characters, purifies our hearts, expands our souls, and makes us more tender and charitable, more worthy to be called the children of God . . . and it is through sorrow and suffering, toil and tribulation, that we gain the education that we come here to acquire and which will make us more like our Father and Mother in heaven.'

"You have sought each other with the right intentions. Although your lives have forever been changed by your past experiences, you have remained strong, courageous, and faithful; you are both survivors!

"You take all the good and bad of the past with you. So share until you understand each other; nourish and heal each other. This is a new beginning of expectations; keep it pure, committed, filled with integrity and respect. Pray together each day and dedicate your lives to the Lord and to each other.

"Do you see your reflections in the mirror behind you?" asked the officiator pointing to the wall-size mirror at one end of the room. "To this point in your lives you've grown separately. That is what you reflect on, learn from, and now put behind you. Looking forward, in the mirror in front of you, is your future—not alone, the two of you together. And you see," the officiator motioned to the mirrored view, "there is no end to it."

Stephanie looked with David at the mirrored illusion of a room without end.

"There is no end to the beauty of your walk together when that walk is coupled with God.

"You know," continued the officiator, "when Thomas Edison decided to light up the city with his electricity, he hooked up two generators to the lights. When he turned the switch, the lights went on but they fluctuated up and down—bright and dim, bright and dim. Sometimes they fluctuated so low, they almost went out. But then he figured out a way to make a machinery shaft that connected the two generators together to stabilize them so they'd pull at the same time—together. As soon as he did that, the lights stopped flickering, they all steadied out and were constant.

"The two of you are the generators for your family. Allow God to remain the stabilizing shaft in your lives. Holding His hand, you can call down the powers of heaven to keep a constant flow of righteous energy in your home. Pull together. Work together. Synchronize your efforts, and as it says in the Doctrine and Covenants, '. . . he that receiveth light, and continueth in God, receiveth more light; and that light groweth brighter and brighter until the perfect day.' (D&C 50:24.)

"David, Stephanie is your friend, she is your partner, your inspiration. Stephanie, David is your strength, your exemplar, your love. You will not miss what you do not know is there! Be diligent to recognize each other's unique gifts. Be sensitive to recognize each other's best qualities. Develop and exercise patience and faith . . ."

David and Stephanie, now sealed in the temple of God for all eternity, stepped out of their car onto the driveway of their new home at the foot of the mountains. Across the valley a single woman had once stopped and sat for a time in silence experiencing a distinct impression that she would some day live at the foot of the distant mountains.

"My mountain, my magnificent mountain," Stephanie said.

David asked, "What? What are you saying?"

Stephanie smiled, "Nothing." She squeezed his hand. "I love you."

A summit, simply a summit I never imagined. What is next? Whatever it is, with God's help I'll claim it, I'll climb it, my mountain.

Author's Note

Today many fraudulent individuals and companies take advantage of others. There are numerous options to follow as you seek companionship. Petition the Lord's aid in recognizing the specific pattern and plan for you. Follow the formula provided by the prophet Joseph Smith in the Doctrine and Covenants 9:8–9: ". . . you must study it out in your mind; then you must ask me [the Lord] if it be right, and if it is right I will cause that your bosom shall burn within you; therefore, you shall feel that it is right. But if it be not right you shall have no such feelings, but you shall have a stupor of thought that shall cause you to forget the thing which is wrong. . . ."

Listen for and ponder the promptings of the Holy Ghost to guide you. Daily express your gratitude to the Lord for your many blessings; fight against discouraging forces, and be determined to accomplish your mission and responsibilities on earth. I promise the Lord hears your prayers, if you sincerely seek Him, and He will triumphantly reward you with specific direction in your life.